Attainment and Executive Functioning in the Early Years

Attainment and Executive Functioning in the Early Years combines knowledge and understanding from research with operational skills from practice in the early years. It presents the development of a sense of self which occurs between birth and five years, the effect of adverse childhood experiences and the link to executive functioning in adulthood.

The book supports the development of expertise which can be applied to enhance inclusive pedagogy, to nurture attainment and to contribute to life-long learning. It explores practice approaches which support children to gain a sense of self, to recognise the needs of others and to achieve fulfilment by operating with purpose. Research is accessed to gain knowledge and understanding of the complex processes which result in a demonstration of executive functioning in childhood.

Attainment and Executive Functioning in the Early Years will be of great interest to academics, researchers and post-graduate students in the fields of early years' care and education. It will also appeal to those working within children's services.

Hazel G. Whitters is a Senior Early Years' Worker and Child Protection Officer in a family centre in Glasgow, Scotland. She has conducted research on the therapeutic relationship in child protection and early intervention.

Routledge Research in Early Childhood Education

This series provides a platform for researchers to present their latest research and discuss key issues in Early Childhood Education.

Books in the series include

Facebook and Beginning Early Childhood Teachers
Tower of Strength or Intimidation?
Sharryn Clarke

Animals in Early Childhood Education
Diahann Gallard

Dance-Play and Drawing as Semiotic Tools for Young Children's Learning
Jan Deans and Susan Wright

Facebook Mentoring and Early Childhood Teachers
The Controversy in Virtual Professional Identity
Sharryn Clarke

Early Childhood Education and Change in Diverse Cultural Contexts
Edited by Chris Pascal, Tony Bertram and Marika Veisson

Early Childhood Care and Education at the Margins
African Perspectives on Birth to Three
Edited by Hasina Banu Ebrahim, Auma Okwany and Oumar Barry

Attainment and Executive Functioning in the Early Years
Research for Inclusive Practice and Lifelong Learning
Hazel G. Whitters

For more information about this series, please visit: www.routledge.com/education/series/RRECE

Attainment and Executive Functioning in the Early Years

Research for Inclusive Practice and Lifelong Learning

Hazel G. Whitters

LONDON AND NEW YORK

First published 2019
by Routledge

2 Park Square, Milton Park, Abingdon, Oxfordshire OX14 4RN

52 Vanderbilt Avenue, New York, NY 10017

Routledge is an imprint of the Taylor & Francis Group, an informa business

First issued in paperback 2020

Copyright © 2019 Hazel G. Whitters

The right of Hazel G. Whitters to be identified as author of this work has been asserted by her in accordance with sections 77 and 78 of the Copyright, Designs and Patents Act 1988.

All rights reserved. No part of this book may be reprinted or reproduced or utilised in any form or by any electronic, mechanical, or other means, now known or hereafter invented, including photocopying and recording, or in any information storage or retrieval system, without permission in writing from the publishers.

Notice:
Product or corporate names may be trademarks or registered trademarks, and are used only for identification and explanation without intent to infringe.

British Library Cataloguing-in-Publication Data
A catalogue record for this book is available from the British Library

Library of Congress Cataloging-in-Publication Data
A catalog record for this book has been requested

ISBN: 978-0-367-14098-4 (hbk)
ISBN: 978-0-367-60656-5 (pbk)

Typeset in Times New Roman
by Apex CoVantage, LLC

I dedicate this book to my husband, John, and my 13 nephews and nieces: John, George and Peter, Dominic and Euan, Joseph, Aidan and Daniel, Mark, Paul and Jennifer, Caroline and Sarah. I have learned so much by watching you grow and develop throughout childhood, and I am proud to see you fulfilling your potential as confident young adults. Thank you!

Contents

Introduction		1
1	The autobiographical sense of self	6
2	Implementation gap and professional development	27
3	Intra-personal and inter-personal communication	38
4	Attainment and executive functioning	66
5	Inter-generational impact and executive functioning	83
	Index	91

Introduction

EF is the abbreviation for *executive functioning* as denoted within academic publications. These two letters represent a concept which lies at the core of every human being, and demonstrates each person's unique contribution to the world. As a practitioner I had not encountered the term "executive functioning" until I returned to part-time post-graduate study at university, 10 years ago. Each evening I would immerse myself in theory and research, and by day I would implement the curriculum, coordinate child protection, teach, care and nurture the next generation of learners. The marriage of studying and practising promotes a deep level of comprehension which grants significance to the minutiae that envelops a child in his or her earliest years. My own EF has certainly increased as a practitioner-researcher.

I have practised for over thirty years in childcare and education in contexts of residential care, primary schools, emergency respite and early years' services. Through countless observations of children I have gained learning and shared laughter, increased comprehension and posed questions and felt excitement laced with positive anticipation. Ultimately I have acquired profound respect for the resilience of children who operate effectively within a vortex of ecological influences.

Development of a sense of the autobiographical self and the ability and capacity to demonstrate executive functioning are integral to attainment from birth throughout a lifespan. The concepts of executive functioning, working memory, shifting and response inhibition are used liberally in academic publications; however educators and parents comprehend a child's sense of self from a different perspective. Practitioners describe self in reference to a child's personality, which determines individuality, and "meeting developmental milestones." Parents use phrases incorporating a descriptor of self which recognises their child's increasing independence, and characteristics, for example, "he knows himself well."

There are many books which describe executive functioning in school children and adolescents with a particular focus upon unsociable actualisation. Readers are taught to adopt practical strategies in response to negative behaviours in the context of curriculum implementation. Generic approaches may support a child to conform to a classroom environment; however the child is learning to inhibit behaviour as opposed to identifying and applying skills which benefit himself and the group. The former is an example of a deficit model of attainment. The child's executive functioning is being curtailed by the educator who focuses upon self-control and minimises the influence from self-regulation.

There are also numerous academic publications accessible as journal articles or briefs which present research on this topic. Research findings and discussion tend to focus upon the neurological system, and the processes which occur within each child during the execution of skills. My experience of practice in the field, and presentations to academics, clearly demonstrates that there still remains a distinct gap between research findings on this topic and application of knowledge within services or the home environment. Research enriches our knowledge as educators, and findings can potentially influence policy; however the optimum effect can only be achieved by considering the implementation gap, by identifying similarities, and divergence and finally by establishing a common bond between strategy which is based upon theory and operational practice.

This book presents development of a rudimentary sense of self which occurs between birth and five years of age, and the links to executive functioning in adulthood which can affect the individual and society. The skill to inhibit and to demonstrate specific behaviours begins to form in the earliest years of childhood through interaction with primary and secondary carers. The child gains understanding of her physical, intellectual, emotional and social self. She takes pride in making an impact upon her world through the use of exploration, recourse to memories, social interaction and regulation of behaviour. Self-regulation is an essential skill for human beings to exist productively, cooperatively and peacefully in our social world as children and adults – in education and leisure, as followers and leaders, as parents and politicians.

Expectations of behaviour within the three stages of adulthood – young, middle age and elderly – have changed over recent years. These changes are due to economic and cultural influences which have resulted in major population mobility within and between countries. It is no longer the norm for adults to live and work in their birth communities. It is no longer the case that unsociable traits and poor decision-making can be absorbed and accepted within a local culture. Each person requires an acute awareness of his inner being, and the ability to demonstrate executive functioning within a multitude of contexts, in order to adapt and to operate effectively in a changing world. The book describes how research links antagonistic behaviour and low achievement to an immature autobiographical self.

Research in neuroscience has increased our comprehension of the significance of learning in the earliest years of childhood, and led to an increase in the allocation of funding to the early years' sector. Financial support, short- and long-term, has extended the provision of services, targeted the development of indoor and outdoor learning environments and influenced training of the workforce. Additionally, society promotes a working culture as representative of effective parenting, and this has led to demand and expansion in childcare and education from birth.

Admission to early years' services is dependent on national and local policies which respond to two categories of need: firstly, day care to enable parents to continue formal education, and ultimately to gain employment; secondly, day care and education to promote family learning in a context of early intervention for our most vulnerable children. Research findings have influenced the creation of early years' curricula, the composition of learning environments, and the promotion of play within inclusive pedagogy. These areas are well supported by the work of previous authors in formats of guidance and multiple course books.

The autobiographical self continues to develop throughout a lifespan, and requires a firm foundation of knowledge and understanding to be established in early childhood. Eight-five percent of UK children attend nursery from the age of three to five years. This figure is currently increasing due to funding for eligible two year olds. The target population of young learners is available, and the workforce has the capacity and motivation to develop their skills. *Attainment and Executive Functioning in the Early Years* does not attempt to replicate the work of past authors. This book aims to upskill practitioners through an increase in understanding of care and education from each child's perspective. The book explores the inner being of a child, and the potential for active participation in learning as the sense of self develops. It promotes comprehension to the reader, in academia and practice, by linking theoretical concepts to common illustrative examples from the daily interactions of the early years' worker. The book is not about an accumulation of strategies by the professional but development of expertise which can be applied to enhance inclusive pedagogy, and to contribute to life-long learning from childhood to adulthood.

Chapter 1, "The autobiographical sense of self," presents knowledge and understanding of the concept of "self" from two different perspectives: research on the biological, intellectual and emotional processes within the first five years of childhood, and daily practice between the child as a developing person and the professional as secondary attachment figure. It has been well established that secure attachment between a child and familiar adult activates the processes associated with learning, and ultimately development. The chapter discusses the five stages of a sense of self in a context of theory illustrated by examples from the child's earliest years. A key issue is the impact of an immature sense of self upon childhood learning, and the accumulative negative effect upon achievement in adulthood.

Chapter 2, "Implementation gap and professional development," contributes to discussion of links between research and practice, by focusing upon policy and theoretical principles. Theory deepens our learning, facilitates the transfer of concepts to different contexts and supports consistent implementation of practice. Principles are the strap-lines from theoretical frameworks. These tenets are composed with diligence, and every word entraps wisdom and encourages the reader to seek out links to further and deeper comprehension. Principles represent findings from research, and the few words of knowledge may be the result of many years of collecting and analysing data in the field.

Matching theory and practice in order to close the implementation gap is not an exact science, and there cannot be a definitive outcome in the early years of human development. The ever-evolving nature of these processes provides the key to professional development and responsive care by promoting life-long learning for the service-provider, as well as the service-user. The issue is illustrated to the reader in a context of the outdoor learning environment: Outdoor Nurseries are current pilot projects and focus for early intervention in Scotland and throughout the world. This chapter includes a section on professional development.

Chapter 3, "Intra-personal and inter-personal communication," explores the link between executive functioning and language. Communication in the format of verbal language or non-verbal means is integral to provide internal scaffolding of information. Positioning of information for use is significant to actualisation and executive functioning. Sorting our knowledge of the world affects its application in response to our needs and others. Our reciprocal interactions with others are dependent on this internal foundation.

Common ground is established between academics, practitioners and parents despite the use of different terminology. The phenomenon of private speech, as termed in research, is discussed alongside the use of current practical strategies of tracking, descriptive praise and finally self-affirmation as applied within services and parenting programmes in the home environment. The context of this chapter includes examples from the pre-verbal developmental stage of childhood, in addition to children who have additional support for learning needs.

Chapter 4, "Attainment and executive functioning," discusses the principles of working memory, response inhibition, self-regulation and task-shifting. Executive functioning can be interpreted in practice as purposeful interaction with a learning environment which involves the use of deep level learning. There are few research studies on executive functioning in early childhood, and this chapter explores the issues in a context of research from the field of neuroscience illustrated by practice examples. Comprehension of the link between executive functioning in childhood and adulthood is significant to strategic and operational planning within services. Partnership-working between parents as primary carers and professionals as secondary carers and educators is highlighted as opportunistic and necessary to equip children to operate effectively within our changing world.

Chapter 5, "Inter-generational impact and executive functioning," refers to recent research and highlights the significance of family learning and early intervention. The relationship with an attachment figure of parent and a potential generational impact upon the child's executive functioning are presented to the reader for consideration.

The chapter presents links between exposure to dysfunctionality in childhood, self-regulatory failure in adults, and mental/physical health conditions. Three levels of stress response are discussed in a context of brain development: positive stress, tolerable stress and toxic stress. The primary outcome of executive functioning is attainment in daily living in addition to achieving educational goals, but it is important to consider the link between crime reduction and the particular skills associated with executive functioning: working memory, self-regulation and task/set-shifting. The final chapter concludes with key messages.

1 The autobiographical sense of self

This chapter presents knowledge and understanding of the concept of "self" from two different perspectives: research on the biological, intellectual and emotional processes within the first five years of childhood and daily practice between the child as a developing person and the professional as secondary attachment figure. It has been well established that secure attachment between a child and familiar adult activates the processes associated with learning, and ultimately development. The impact of an immature sense of self upon childhood learning is presented and the accumulative negative effect upon achievement in adulthood as the child progresses through his or her learning journey.

EXAMPLE FROM PRACTICE

Self at three years of age

The sky was heavy, and a yellow glow cast an ominous appearance upon the land-scape. Large raindrops pattered steadily onto the winter leaves which carpeted the pine and deciduous woods. The regular beating against the decaying vegetation created a musical prelude which locals would recognise as forecasting a storm. These woods were nestled in an inner city green space in Scotland which had been preserved between the concrete swimming-pool and the local police station.

In a clearing there were obvious signs of activity. Brightly coloured chiffon scarves were tied to the trees, and represented a visual boundary between safe and unsafe play areas, as determined by council policies and procedures. A group of nursery children were crouched under a large umbrella of a sycamore tree and waited expectantly for the next adventure in their Outdoor Nursery.

A four year old boy asked his younger peer for help in lifting a rotten log. The child obviously had a plan. Active play began, and the three year old helper wrapped his arms impulsively around the middle section of the log. The leader in this imaginative episode shook his head vigorously and pointed to the end of the log: balance, weight, logistics and delegation had been carefully considered. Three year old Fraser quickly changed tactics, and grasped the log-end, watching and wondering as he copied the four year old who was performing an executive function (purposeful interaction with a learning environment). Fraser's ability to task-shift was clear.

Complementary actions encompassed cooperative play between the children. The two friends dragged the log around the woodland area, looking at each other and laughing in recognition of their competent teamwork. I gave the boys a high-five hand-clap, and commented on their achievements.

Forward planning through the use of "working memory," "verbal and non-verbal communication," "task-shifting," "self-regulation" of physical prowess, "social interaction," "goal recognition" and "executive functioning" were positive outcomes in this little clearing in the city of Glasgow, on a rainy day in February. The sense of self at three years of age.

Research and Practice

Research can be challenging to use within the daily practice of care and education of our youngest children. Extracting meaning from research findings in order to enhance the implementation of daily nursery routines, or to support interaction with a distressed parent or to inform collegiate discussions in child protection is difficult. I often find that consideration of the issues by using the "bottom up approach," as described by social policy makers, provides realism and connections in attempts to close the implementation gap between academia and practice.

We share a goal of caring for and educating each child to achieve potential. "Potential" is a powerful word in our language and implies self-worth, immediate impact value, and hope for a positive future. Research identifies that "actualization" (practical outcome) of potential is determined by a multitude of internal and external factors. Policy demands and expects positive outcomes and clearly promotes that supporting achievement of potential for each child is the only goal for services; however, clarification of this result is ill-defined.

Research can present a finding in the context of an executive summary or a mandate inserted within policy, but practitioners have an inherent framework for implementation which needs to be fulfilled. Significant aspects being, Why? What? How? When?

The formal view of practice is outcome-led. The practitioner's view is child-led responsive care. "Implementation gap" is a common term which is used to describe a weak transfer of knowledge and understanding from academic research to direct practice. I have often felt that a more apt descriptor would be an "implementation barrier," which is constructed by the use of theoretical terms as applicable to academia. This obstruction to information sharing encompasses the use of concepts which fit neatly within the researcher's brief. Research is challenging to comprehend from the practitioner's perspective.

Alternatively, the difficulty in re-interpreting practice observations into the format of research data may result in minimisation of the effect upon development and of progress in this field. Practice responds to needs and behaviours of individuals, young and old, who operate in a vortex of unpredictable ecological influences. Responsive practice cannot follow generic rules, and there is often a disconnection between recommendations which are based upon research findings and face-to-face implementation in real time, one human being to another.

As a practitioner-researcher I can view issues from each of these perspectives. I commenced post-graduate study after 25 years of practising, and I quickly realised that my practice could be transformed by accessing the deepest level of learning which emerges from research. My research also benefited from practical experience in understanding people, vulnerable or resilient, who operate day by day through life's challenges and successes. This section will commence by exploring research, policy and practice, and presenting the reader with an opportunity to consider the issues.

Stages of self

Research identifies that development of a human being, at the stage of conception to birth, is a naturally supported process which is led by genetic pathways. This premise of life creates common ground between the academic and parent. Trevarthan and Aitken (2001) describe maternal tissues embracing the tiny embryo. A mother-to-be will visualise her baby, in utero, and send love, care and expectations of achievement to the tiny developing person throughout pregnancy.

The foetus is enveloped by opportunities in the form of genetic influences which may or may not be activated in the period of gestation. There are two phases for the foetus termed "emergent" and "development." Stern (1998) also refers to the emergent sense of self which forms in the two months after birth. The impact from uni-directional and bi-directional influences contributes to the unique presentation of each new baby in our world.

An understanding of self can be portrayed on a simplistic level but requires further exploration in order to fully appreciate the complexities of human development. There are five recognised stages: physical agent, social agent, teleological agent, intentional mental agent, and autobiographical self (Trevarthan & Aitken, 2001). Achievement of these stages of human development occurs sequentially, and the average child will gain comprehension of the autobiographical self at approximately five years of age (Miell, 1995). This comprehension must be regarded as rudimentary as the sense of self changes in accordance with maturity and experience.

Practice and research shows that development does not always occur in the expected linear manner which relates to developmental norms, and the five stages are inter-dependent. For example the new-born period is regarded as the first 28 days of life (Colombo & Horowitz, 1987), and within these four calendar weeks a new baby has the capacity to gain knowledge and experiential learning of the first three stages of self. By the fourth month an infant has the potential to comprehend self as an intentional mental agent. Whitebread and Basilio (2011) suggest that these young babies of a few months old can realise personal impact upon the proximal environment which is demonstrated through their desire to repeat actions or to have actions repeated.

1. Physical agent

The new-born baby commences on a life-long journey of physical exploration and bodily responses to learning environments. The acts of seeking knowledge, interpreting situations and reacting or interacting by using motor skill provide a child with a framework of the physical self. This framework emerges upon satisfaction of need and experiential play. Knowledge of the physical self includes application of acquired skills and potential for development in the context of ability to forward plan. This operational base is essential to maintain health and safety of self. A baby and young child continue to be dependent on adult support for many years, and potentially throughout life; however, an increasing self-awareness will commence from birth.

Physical reaction to immediate danger in the proximal environment is initially instinctive. Over time, use of the inner working model leads to re-configuration of prior knowledge, and instinctive reaction is transformed into informed action. The inner working model can be regarded as a personal reference framework, and encompasses information, understanding, attitudes, values and principles which are used to function effectively within the world of child or adult.

EXAMPLE FROM PRACTICE

Self at one week old

One week old baby Hope is crying after her feed. The young mother supports Hope's body in an upright sitting position upon her knee, and she rubs her back rhythmically. The baby's back is rounded, and her heavy head dips forward – neck muscles are forming but not yet able to maintain a mid-line position. The teenager's hexagonal bangles create a regular musical clink as she moves her hand up and down her little baby's pink woollen jumper. Hope wriggles and cries. She does not demonstrate any acceptance of this soothing action as an appropriate response to her needs. Maternal grandmother leans across her daughter and scoops the tiny grandchild competently into her arms. She declares confidently, "That's a cry for a change of nappy!"

The grandmother turned her thoughts to the infant, and started to converse by tracking the baby's needs alongside her reactions, "You're so upset because you need a change. Is your nappy wet? Yes it is, and you cried to get attention. You are a clever girl. I am going to take off your wet nappy, and you'll feel so much better. There, there, you can stop crying now. You know that you are fine, and you're smiling at gran."

The matriarch of this family sits little Hope across one arm, and uses her other arm as alternative back-rest to support her granddaughter's body. She rocked her gently, up and down, instinctively following the beat of a human heart. Hope responds and relaxes – a "physical agent" and early stages of gaining social agency.

These conversations, and actions take place in every household with a young baby. It may seem like an inconsequential interlude in the daily routine of baby-care, but this grandmother is delivering essential information, and understanding to her grandchild which supports her mentalisation of inner self in the context of the external world.

What does this mean in theory and practice?

Assuaging a physical need is paramount for the young baby in her earliest weeks, and inherent instinct is to seek help until an appropriate response is given. Parents often refer to the use of guesswork in the initial hours, days and weeks of parenthood, but over time primary carers gain a vast array of knowledge and understanding of their child's needs, wants and interests. Reflective responding to a young baby can lead to inter-subjectivity which is based upon a secure attachment relationship (Trevarthan & Aitken, 2001). These authors describe this function as potentially available from birth as a baby is motivated to communicate with others at an emotional level.

Research by Whitebread and Basilio (2011) indicated that care routines support the developing infant to modulate her emotional responses. Additionally, consistent periods of sleep and wakefulness initiate the foundations for emotional balance which can contribute to learning throughout childhood. Parental experience and research (Byrne & Horowitz, 1981) confirm that soothing, stroking and rocking are natural and effective approaches to support a young infant to de-stress, and to regulate her emotional expression until the status of alert-awareness is achieved – the readiness to learn.

First and third generation of a family

- Grandmother establishes a familial dyad through physical closeness and handling of baby Hope.
- Grandmother is creating, maintaining, and re-affirming a secure attachment relationship which relates to her predictable, consistent and timely responses to the baby's needs, and wants. Timely is a significant aspect as inability to self-regulate negative emotions can rapidly induce stress in a young baby.
- The circumstances of attending to a young baby's physical needs present ideal opportunities to capitalise on the delivery of emotional support and to promote communication. For example, as Hope lies on her back upon a changing mat she has opportunities to give eye contact, to mirror actions of the adult, to absorb the explicit connection between movement and sound.
- Grandmother naturally expresses links between the baby's needs, her responses and her grand-daughter's emotions – the beginning of emotional literacy for this new-born.
- Grandmother unknowingly creates a link between secure attachment, physical wellbeing and mental stabilisation – an emerging knowledge base for Hope's development of resilience, and self-regulation.
- The baby is exposed to the culture of family during these moments of care by a primary adult within a home environment – beliefs, attitude and values.
- Grandmother is also consolidating the attachment relationship with her teenage daughter, in the role of Hope's mother: role-modelling good parenting practice, nurturing, teaching and establishing patterns of care for the next generation which will contribute to a framework for living, relevant to this particular family.
- These early daily routines, which incur direct signalling of need and personalised responsive care by attachment figures, are significant events in a child's developmental pathway.

2. Social agent

Research (Bowlby, 1979) has established that secure attachment to a primary carer is an essential condition for a child to achieve social agency. Attachment theory has been clearly communicated to professionals in the last twenty years through research, training, policy, curricula and practice guidance. The secure adult-child relationship is a necessary foundation for the development of a sense of the autobiographical self. Fonagy (1999) described emotional regulation as evolving throughout the earliest years, and beyond, within the dyad of a primary carer. This author highlighted a link between classification of attachment in childhood and the same classification in the adult years. A long-term research study of 17,000 participants, termed The California Adverse Childhood Experience Study, indicated long-term outcomes of insecure attachment in the early years as mental health, crime and low attainment (Sroufe et al., 2005, 2006).

Each one of us has a different personality, needs and interests which affect our expression of the social self. Descriptors of extrovert, introvert, observer, activator, leader or follower imply that humans have established a norm in this area of development against which social interaction is judged. I believe that there is a perfect niche for everyone in the world, and provision of optimum conditions, in the form of attachment relationships, will allow the unique sense of social self to develop. Achievement of a social self cannot be measured or predicted, but executive functioning is a recognisable outcome. Executive functioning can be summarised as purposeful interaction with the world (Whitters, 2018).

A baby who is feeling hungry, wet, lonely or tired will instinctively cry for support in order that these needs and emotions are responded to. The baby aspires to a status of comfort and safety. Research (Trevarthan & Aitken, 2001) indicates that new-born babies will also demonstrate motivation to gain a relationship which does not relate to their immediate biological needs. These authors describe these processes of relationship-building as specific to human beings although reference is also made to self-awareness in animals, reminiscent of the early stages of the autobiographical sense of self.

The question that readers should consider is the link to the child's sense of social agency.

- Does this motivation become active only after the biological needs are satisfied; therefore, is there a timely link for intervention between physical wellbeing and promotion of emotional and social care?
- Do these actions initiate the creation of a social self?
- Is the sense of social self already established at birth; therefore, do positive or negative interactions with others enhance or perhaps diminish the baby's understanding of social agency?

Readers will have beliefs on these points which relate to expertise in academia, practice or parenting role. I belief that motivation and inherent skills, in the form of attachment cues from baby to parent, indicate that an elementary sense of social self already exists at birth.

EXAMPLE FROM PRACTICE

Self at birth

A new-born baby can be observed blinking in the first few moments of arrival, opening and closing his eyes, initially instinctively as a reaction to the bright hospital birthing lights but then a determination can be observed within this tiny person, a motivation to focus upon the new world and emerging awareness of the effect from the external environment upon himself. He shivers as the first draught touches his skin, and he retracts as a tiny finger is enveloped by the stitching in a hospital blanket. A full body reaction as fine motor skills within a physical sense of self are not yet established. He pushes out his tongue – a familiar comforting skill which he has mastered in utero, "a physical agent."

It seems that the baby is trying to make an emotional connection during his first transition as he enters the world. This proximal world is a city maternity hospital which is described as offering a state of the art approach to welcoming the next generation, but the new-born infant exists within a tiny micro-system: mother and child. The mother instinctively welcomes her son by touching, talking and nurturing, and the baby demonstrates a stillness, a listening body and an awareness of input from another being – a physical agent in the initial stages of social agency.

It could be said that self-regulation is occurring from this point. Blinking, trying to focus, hearing and responding by momentarily pausing – the newborn baby shows an awareness of an external influence, and a desire to seek out more information. He has a readiness to learn.

The teenage mother is also commencing a learning journey, and she is led by maternal instinct triggered with the influx of hormones during this momentous event. The advent of parenthood is regarded as a sensitive, opportune period for acquisition of knowledge and understanding.

Dad is twenty years old. He is tired and thirsty, and out of his common comfort zone of male friends and football chat. The young dad stretches his arms high above the birthing scene, exhausted by the process, but empowered and motivated by the positivity and praise from hospital staff in his moment of fatherhood. His outward stance of pride belies the nervous apprehension which every father experiences at this time.

Dad leans towards his new family, and says "Cuddle up with baby Alfie, and I'll send a photo to gran on Facebook – she'll like that." A simple comment which is repeated many times over in every maternity suite throughout the world, affirming the baby's place within a family unit, widening his micro-system minutes after birth. His appointed name reflects the young age-group of his parents, and the electronic medium which is accessed to announce his birth creates an instantaneous impact via social media – placing this little human being within a context of living in the 21st century.

Research shows us that the effects from epigenetics are apparent at this moment: influences from family and community in the form of expectations, cultural practices, and biological needs. Aspirations, hopes and dreams begin to have a life-long impact upon this tiny child of a few minutes old. This is the world of Alfie.

What does this mean in theory and practice?

Over fifty years ago Wolff (1965) conducted research on the behaviour of neonatal infants, and described an infant's "attentive state" as his ability to show adaptive responses to the proximal environment. Wolff also applied the term "alert-inactivity" to represent the physical state of a neonate immediately before she demonstrated responsive behaviour: the baby is relaxed, her skin is a healthy pink colouration, she has a resting heartbeat, and her eyes are wide. This term continues to be applied in current practice (Stern, 1998).

Research in the intervening years has given greater understanding to practitioners and academics regarding development in the neonatal stage. The concept of "developmental plasticity" provides the rationale for Wolff's description of attentive state, and refers to the ability and capacity of human beings to adapt to social and physical environments. Many examples of the need for this adaptation can be given from the birth of Alfie. Baby Alfie spent his first 48 hours in a single maternity room accompanied by his mother and father. Alfie experienced, and adapted to, unpredictable and contrasting sensory stimulation from a multitude of sources.

- The visual stimulus from bright fluorescent day-time lighting or calming effect of dimmed night-lights in accordance with hospital ward protocol.
- The sound of his mother's voice, as first heard through the womb-wall pre-birth, gave a consistent and familiar auditory back-drop, but was accompanied by spontaneous excited male and female voices during visiting hours.
- Alfie was bottle-fed by his mother or father, and he became aware of the smell of sterilising agent and a link to milk, but he could also smell his mother's breast-milk during her feeding sessions.
- Alfie's skin and head were stimulated and nurtured through cuddling "kangaroo-style" by both parents. The warmth and nurturing in this skin to skin contact contrasted sharply to the ambience of the hospital

cot, in which he was surrounded by cool cotton bedding, and protected by a little woollen cap upon his head.

After two days in hospital Alfie entered the micro-system of his home environment which encompassed influences from the local community. Alfie's world has changed, and he is exposed to patterns of living and interactions based upon the developing attachment relationship with his parents and extended family.

Attachment

Twenty years ago research identified the attachment relationship as a key factor in inter-generational transmission of positive or negative environmental effects (Fonagy, 1999). Brain development is influenced by external factors from the proximal and distal environments, in addition to internal factors, for example, emotions, cognitive processes and a genetic developmental blue-print.

The human central nervous system has "neuroplasticity" which supports structural and consequentially functional changes and which has been linked with our responses to environments (Moore et al., 2017). Responses relate to actions, behaviour and emotions. Plasticity refers to potential for change which may be positive and impact beneficially upon development, but negative outcomes can also occur due to adversities.

Epigenetics

"Epigenetic change" describes the result of the interaction between all these sources. Epigenetic changes can actually be inherited from parent to child with positive or negative effects. For example, parents often replicate their own childhood experiences in providing a home learning environment, the use of parenting style and potential punitive measures regarding a child's behaviour, and development of an attachment relationship. A child's insecure attachment develops in a context of a non-responsive primary carer, which is a common inter-generational effect of adversities. Research has shown that the child's survival techniques will take precedence over accessing developmental opportunities in a negative, chaotic lifestyle (US Department of Health & Human Services, 2011). Practice responds to these circumstances through the use of early intervention for families, which often encompasses three generations, in addition to post-crisis intervention.

Epigenetic change in one generation can become the norm for a family, and this cultural and environmental knowledge can be passed to subsequent generations. Parents will often comment anecdotally and reveal with a little reticence that their actions and approaches to child-rearing are similar to their own parents.

Guidance notes and curricula (Department for Education & Skills, 2000; Scottish Government, 2010; Surestart, 2002) are based upon understanding from The Bio-Ecological Theory of Human Development (Bronfenbrenner, 2006). Information is presented to practitioners in the form of potential influences upon development; therefore, it is essential that early years workers are supported to interpret this knowledge into understanding which is applicable to each child and his ecological circumstances. Epigenetics is an area of human development in which research and practice can inform one another. Population mobility throughout the world will potentially be an influential and unpredictable factor, cross-culturally and across nations. A positive outcome of epigenetics is a rich foundation for human attainment.

3. Teleological agent

Teleological agency is the art of understanding and applying the principles of cause and effect. The theory of mind requires profound understanding of these principles, and subsequently impacts upon behaviour management, self-regulation, cooperative imaginative play, team work in adulthood and sustainability of adult partnerships within the wider society. Reflective capacity emerges alongside theory of mind which subsequently supports demonstration of empathy, responses to attachment and relational cues in the context of family, work and leisure. This foundation of noticing, controlling and using your impact upon the world is an essential step to enable progress to the next stage of self: the intentional mental agent. Researchers have identified this ability in toddlers aged 12–18 months (Whitebread & Basilio, 2011).

EXAMPLE FROM PRACTICE

Self at 30 months old

Nuo Ying is 30 months old. She runs into nursery and stops at the far wall. Nuo Ying turns around and surveys her play-space. This little girl's body stance portrays a sense of ownership – feet are firmly planted on the ground creating a broad and steady viewpoint, Nuo Ying's hands are held in an open position which indicates her confidence and potential for use, her fingers dance against her sides in anticipation, her shoulders are back and her head held high in mid-line. Nuo Ying wears an over-sized yellow hair-bow – following the same trend as her peers in nursery – and this hair adornment

The autobiographical sense of self 17

bobs up and down as the child looks around her domain, noticing, considering and choosing.

There is a wooden frame in the playroom with multiple small compartments which each contain a different receptacle: pink, blue, yellow and green wicker baskets, an empty biscuit tin with a picture of a snowman, smooth cotton long-life bags, rough but warm woollen draw-string bags, and cardboard boxes – large, tiny, square and rectangular, with and without the additional gift of parcel tape. Each container has a hidden wonder inside, attractive to find, and easy to access but challenging for little problem-solvers.

Nuo Ying notices a new addition in the top-most compartment: six chunky coloured pencil-cases. These receptacles had been purchased from a stationery shop but they were designed perfectly for exploratory play by potential teleological agents. Each pencil-case has a vibrant colour and an easy-to-grasp zip – an essential feature in the early days of curiosity. Nuo Ying stretches to reach her goal, and gains the target, which is an electric blue pencil-case. She shakes it. A key worker has hidden little items inside the case, carefully wrapped in tissue-paper to create a tantalising unidentifiable sound. She reviews and reflects. This learner considers, "Do I need help or not? Can I balance and use my fine motor skills? Is there something inside that I cannot see?" Extrapolation of knowledge, forward thinking, if this . . . then that . . . a teleological agent.

This 30 month old girl demonstrates awareness of her own physical sense of self: motor skills, spatial knowledge, balance, the potential output required to open the pencil-case, and her ability to function purposefully to achieve a goal. Planning, predicting one's own impact upon the world – the early stages of becoming an intentional mental agent.

Nuo Ying sits down in one movement – this physical skill is unique to our youngest children, and as adults we can forget that ground-level is the preferred play-ground for children. Zip is open and contents exposed. Within seconds Nuo Ying's own goal has been achieved. It is a different goal to the expectation of her key worker but the child is satisfied and quickly discards the pencil-case behind her back. Nuo Ying is currently developing her understanding of self as a teleological agent. She demonstrated an intense few moments of maturity in planning, predicting and confirming. Thereafter this 30 month old reverted to a younger stage of development by discarding the pencil-case behind her back which was reminiscent of a six-month old without comprehension of object permanency. Objects dropped quickly or discarded behind a child will not be retained in working memory.

The key worker reflects upon Nuo Ying's skills, and records the information rapidly in bullet-points on a sticky note. Practitioners are competent recorders of this type of information which is gleaned throughout the nursery day. The sticky notes will be transferred into accurate observational accounts of the little girl's developmental stage, and related to current curriculum in due course.

What does this mean in theory and practice?

Mentalisation

The basis of this theory is simple but complex – comprehending and accepting that other people may have different views to your own. Friends, family, colleagues or strangers may interpret and react to our shared world from a different perspective. As adults we continue to struggle "to see the world as others see it." We wonder why our fellow human beings cannot understand our point of view, and we are puzzled about the occurrence of misunderstandings in the workplace. Differences of opinion in workplaces are often linked in a generic manner to a lack of effective communication. It may well be that an immaturity in understanding the theory of mind is a contributing factor to these disagreements.

This inter-subjective mentalising process was referred to by the philosopher Hegel (1997) over two hundred years ago. Researchers recently described mentalisation as an inter-personal strategy which supports physical and social development and requires the use of imagination in comprehending the thoughts and intentions of other people (Fonagy et al., 2007). Patterns of behaviour emerge which support the child to represent herself alongside her feelings and to recognise a social context. These patterns are initially based upon role-modelling by the primary carer, and over time, the child internally organises these experiences from a subjective perspective which reflects her personality, needs and interests. A parent or carer will use verbal and non-verbal communication which facilitates the child's creation of mentalising models, and informs her increasing comprehension of links between emotions and actions of self and others.

Maturity in this stage is integral to promote understanding of self as an intentional mental agent. Firstly, a child gains comprehension of herself as a social agent who operates with one or more people in the context of culture and contextual boundaries. Secondly, a child gains comprehension of herself as an intentional mental agent who has different opinions, actions, emotions and potentially intentions towards others or the environment.

Learning takes time. It is a complex accumulative process which requires repetition at lower and higher levels of functioning. Each child has a particular learning style, learning needs which can be relevant to a point in time or short-term or long-term learning needs, interests and personal motivators.

Children will develop progressively but may also return to an earlier stage of the sense of self during exploration, learning and consolidation of knowledge in their pathway to achievement.

The principles of cause and effect have high importance in the development of physical skills, intellectual achievement and operating as a social agent in a local and broad context. Executive functioning in the fields of literacy and mathematics throughout our lives is based upon this foundation of teleological agency: looking forward, imagining what is not yet known, having the confidence to seek and to follow through tentative ideas.

I often consider the privileged perspective of a practitioner in the field of early years. We observe human development slowly unfolding as each child's exploration of his world informs our interpretation. Our comprehension of the link between research and practice soars as we witness human attainment from birth throughout childhood.

4. Intentional mental agent

Our brain development is affected by our emotional reactions, and the physiological functioning of our bodies, for example, metabolic, cardiovascular and musculoskeletal systems (Moore et al., 2017). Many of our biological functions and behaviours are controlled by instinctive reflexes, although some reactions can be overcome in social contexts, as self-regulation develops. A child undergoes multiple levels of learning in order to achieve maturity in the sense of self which enables him to understand his impact upon the world. This comprehension of intentional mental agency can only be known to another being through observing the child's actions, contextualising the child's emotions, interpreting the child's direct or indirect communication and noticing his executive functioning.

EXAMPLE FROM PRACTICE

Daily transition: home to service

9.15 a.m. in the family centre on a winter's morning. Four year old Duncan and his mother, Stacey, enter the playroom. His circumstances are typical of many service-users. Duncan lives with his mother and grandmother but he is encompassed within the protection of social services due to physical and emotional neglect. Duncan is currently "a looked after child" – on the local authority child protection register.

I move forward to welcome this vulnerable family, and I observe that four year old Duncan is clinging onto his mother's legs and stretching for her hand. Stacey responds by holding her hands high in the air and asking staff to take Duncan into the room. I bend down and touch Duncan's hand gently – the tactility creating a bridge to remind this little boy of our attachment, key worker and child. Duncan transfers his grasp from mother to myself, leans against me momentarily then he runs quickly into the den area.

The nursery den is a pop-up tent: an artefact which has transformed playrooms and school nurture-rooms by providing areas of calm, areas to relax, and areas to escape from visible or invisible sources of stress. Pop-up tents are easily transportable, and the brightly coloured material has been covered creatively by a staff member in pastel shades of Indian silk to shield tired eyes from the fluorescent lights in our playroom. A large square cushion provides a comforting safe haven for Duncan and prevents the pop-up tent from collapsing inwards during the quick entry by this angry little boy.

Primary carer's reaction to adversities

I acknowledged that Stacey was feeling upset, and I offered support. Stacey informed me that her washing machine was not working! Broken household appliances affect each one of us, and impinge negatively upon our familiar daily routines of living. Our predictable structure for the day can easily be upturned; however for families who operate in a context of child protection, which includes unannounced visits by services, then this additional adversity can take priority over a child's needs. Duncan's transition from his mother's care into nursery today was difficult, and his behaviour immediately gave me insight into his emotional wellbeing and potential capacity to play and to retain learning.

Child's interests and attachment figure

Stacey left quickly, and I sat outside the den as I talked quietly to Duncan. I opened a book in the entrance and faced the pages towards Duncan. He was lying prone and hiding his eyes which is a typical position of a child with low resilience. I voiced a few questions out loud about the story-line, and Duncan raised his head with interest. A few minutes later the four year old was sitting cross-legged, holding the book, and asking me to turn each page. I noticed the intense gaze in his eyes as the dinosaurs walked between the pages. Suddenly another boy attempted to push Duncan by diving forward as if the blue cushion was a pool of water. Duncan hit his peer, and protested loudly, then he left the den abruptly.

Positive reinforcement of self

I observed Duncan run over to the garage and car table, and he stood on one leg, hopping and balancing. I showed Duncan that I noticed this skill by tracking his movements, and commenting that he looked proud. Duncan continued to balance on alternate legs, and smiled tentatively at me.

Child's reaction to adversities

As I observed I noticed several features of Duncan's play relating to sensory exploration, social rules and interpretation of his sense of self:

- *He chose cars within easy reach, and did not attempt to walk around the play table to gain access to additional vehicles. Duncan was restricting play in order to maintain his status quo – vigilance is easier from a stationary position – "self regulation to maintain safety."*
- *He examined each car with two hands, spinning the wheels and trying to open the car doors. Duncan was demonstrating forward planning, and potential imaginative play – "early stages of teleological agency."*
- *He gained great satisfaction as he made the cars collide with a loud bang. Duncan was affirming his control of the learning environment by recognising his predicted actions, and goal – "repetition and working memory."*
- *Two peers joined the play at the opposite side of the table.*
- *These two boys talked to one another with enthusiasm and agreed that the cars could go up the slope, and down the ramp. Cooperative and imaginative play was apparent in seconds – "sense of intentional mental agency."*
- *Duncan stopped his play, and observed. He glanced from one child to the other, and I noticed that Duncan's eyes were wide open as if he was seeking knowledge and understanding of this peer dyad. He laughed when the two boys laughed. His hands were moving slightly as he mirrored the movements of his peers. Duncan's feet edged forward, and suddenly he pushed a car up the ramp. The two friends reprimanded his action. Duncan swept several cars onto the floor, and ran to the climbing frame. He kept his back to the scene of adversity.*

Duncan was obviously interested in creating friendships but he did not appear to have the relational skills necessary. Once again Duncan had chosen flight as a reaction to the creation of peer relationships which consolidated this little boy's barrier to achievement of potential.

What does this mean in theory and practice?

Adversities can dramatically affect this pivotal stage of development. Confirmation and continuation of a child's impact upon his proximal and potentially distal environments requires responsive care-giving and secure attachment. Internally a child makes a superficial judgement and acknowledgement of his influence which is confirmed, rejected or minimised externally by peer and adult responses. The child's motivation to seek out learning, to build self-esteem, and to gain resilience are affected by reactions to his overtures. These external responses are based upon expectations from different people – individuals or groups who apportion value to the child's impact upon the world, for example:

- Impact of child's actions and emotions upon his development – progressive or regressive
- Impact of child's actions and emotions upon siblings or peers – sociable or unsociable
- Impact of child's actions and emotions upon adults – positive or negative.
- Representation of the family values and attitude in child's actions and emotions – culturally acceptable or unacceptable.
- Representation of values and attitudes in child's actions and emotions which relate to the immediate social setting, for example nursery or school – conforming to expectations or not.

Our sense of worth is heavily influenced by the reactions of others, and in the child's earliest years, the responsive care from a primary carer has the greatest impact. Reactions can be presented explicitly to the baby/infant in the form of verbal communication or direct action, and implicitly as emotions and body language. The outcome is ultimately social acceptance or rejection within a particular micro-system. Fonagy et al. (2007) link social competence with cultural knowledge which is transferred through each generation and within a community. The child will be equipped, cognitively and culturally, to operate effectively in a local context. Steady progress in achieving a sense of the autobiographical self is linked to epigenetics, and learning opportunities which are presented to the baby/infant within a context of secure attachment perpetuate the developmental cycle. Alternatively, negative experiences will delay, restrict or change the infant's understanding of self.

5. Autobiographical self

The sense of self continues to develop and to mature throughout our lifespans, and impacts directly upon executive functioning.

EXAMPLE FROM PRACTICE

Role-modelling and positive reinforcement

A staff member started to encourage preparation for snack-time. Many children responded quickly and eagerly by moving the little red chairs into their places, cleaning tables with a sense of importance, and putting toys away while sorting, and remembering, or asking for advice, "Where does this go?"

I noted that three year old Dominique kept her back to the activity in the playroom which was created by her peers. I approached the diminutive child and gently brushed her fair plaited hair aside. I gained eye-contact, albeit reluctantly after I touched her face. Dominique accepted my offer of teamwork, and I quickly accessed one of the small empty baskets which were scattered around the playroom as prompts to support knowledge and skills associated with "tidy-up time."

I demonstrated "toys away" by dropping some yellow bricks into a basket with a resounding clatter. The three year learner copied my actions, and we rapidly developed a rhythm of turn-taking which was clarified by the noise of goal achievement. Dominique and I happily inter-changed the roles of helper, and being helped as we counted bricks and named colours. Developmental opportunities can easily be opportunistic, and I capitalised upon this child's readiness to learn.

Supporting development of self

A young boy approached our work-team with some bricks. Dominique's brows furrowed and she shouted "no," but listened, and accepted the conditions of negotiation. I held the basket as the two peers stood on either side of me and put the toys away. Turn-taking by Dominique had abruptly ended as the boy entered the scene, and parallel play emerged. I gave the two youngsters a hug, and thanked them by using descriptive praise, and the universal thumbs up!

Demonstrating an understanding of self

As Dominique walked forward to wash her hands before snack-time I noticed that her body language reflected the positive effects of achievement. Her head was held high, braided plaits bounced on her slim shoulders, her arms were swinging freely, and she walked with purpose and an end goal established. Today this three year old had complete understanding and acceptance of the nursery routines, and for a few moments at least,

Dominque's world was good as she demonstrated her emerging sense of autobiographical self.

What does this mean in theory and practice?

Having a "sense" of the autobiographical self is an accurate representation of this status. It could be argued that elementary comprehension of autobiographical self is only achieved if the child perceives that there is a subjective and objective interpretation of her impact upon the world. She appreciates that her operational contribution will be interpreted by others, and the outcome may differ from her own interpretation of self. A definitive stage is realised by the young child in her emerging awareness that she can function independently of her primary carer, but the underlying necessity is the emotional ethereal bond which underpins the sense of self and the ability and capacity to demonstrate executive functioning.

Scaffolding

Daniels (2001) proposes different interpretations of the term "scaffolding":

- Support is given to a child in the initial stages of task performance and withdrawn thereafter
- Support is given in the form of collaboration between child and adult following a child's initial attempts during task performance
- The adult or "experienced person" constructs support in the form of one-way scaffolding which is presented to a child to use in task performance, and it is usually specific and instructional rather than general guidance
- The promotion of creativity and meaning of a task to the child as opposed to instructional guidance

Another interpretation of scaffolding is the adult's understanding of a child's emotional status and the adult's demonstration of reflective responding which promotes emotional wellbeing, and potentially motivation and incentive to achieve the task. Evidence of each definition can be found in practice today as early years' workers access different approaches to respond to each child's learning needs.

References

Bowlby, J. (1979). *The making and breaking of affectional bonds*. (pp. 13, 29–30, 41–45, 84–87, 124–127, 134, 154–155, 165–174, 181–187). Abingdon: Routledge.

The autobiographical sense of self 25

Bronfenbrenner, U., & Morris, P. A. (2006). The bioecological model of human development. In W. Damon & R. M. Lerner (Eds.), *Handbook of child psychology, volume 1* (pp. 796–798, 800, 810–815). Hoboken, NJ: Wiley & Sons.

Byrne, J. M., & Horowitz, F. D. (1981). Rocking as soothing intervention: The influence of direction and type of movement. *Infant Behaviour and Development*. Retrieved on 6 March, 2018, from www.sciencedirect.com/science/article/pii/S0163638381800240?via%3Dihub

Colombo, J., & Horowitz, J. (1987). Behavioural state as a lead variable in neonatal research. *Merrill-Palmer Quarterly, volume 33, number 4*. Retrieved on 6 March, 2018, from www.jstor.org/stable/23086402

Daniels, H. (2001). *Vygotsky and pedagogy*. Abingdon: RoutledgeFalmer.

Department for Education & Skills. (2000). *The early years' foundation stage: Effective practice: Parents as partners*. London: HMSO.

Fonagy, P. (1999). Transgenerational consistencies of attachment: A new theory. *Dallas Society for Psychoanalytic Psychology*. Retrieved on 16 December, 2013, from www.dspp.com/papers/fonagy2.htm

Fonagy, P., Gergely, G., & Target, M. (2007). The parent-infant dyad and the construction of the subjective self. *Journal of Child Psychology and Psychiatry, volume 48, number 3/4*, 288–328. Oxford: Blackwell Publishing.

Hegel, G. W. F. (1997). *Phenomenology of spirit*. Retrieved on 28 March, 2018, from https://plato.stanford.edu/entries/hegel

Miell, D. (1995). The development of self. In P. Barnes (Ed.), *Personal, social and emotional development of children* (pp. 190–201). Blackwell: Open University Press.

Moore, T., Arefadib, N., Deery, A., & West, S. (2017). *The first thousand days: An evidence paper*. Retrieved on 30 September, 2017, from www.rch.org.au/cch

Scottish Government. (2010). *Pre-birth to three: Positive outcomes for Scotland's children and families*. Edinburgh: Scottish Government.

Sroufe, L. A., Egeland, B., Carlson, E., & Collins, W. A. (2005). *The development of the person: The Minnesota study of risk and adaptation from birth to adulthood*. New York: The Guilford Press.

Sroufe, L. A., Egeland, B., Carlson, E., & Collins, W. A. (2006). Placing early attachment experiences in developmental context. In K. E. Grossman, K. Grossman & E. Watters (Eds.), *Attachment from infancy to adulthood: The major longitudinal studies* (pp. 48–70). New York: The Guilford Press.

Stern, D. N. (1998). *The interpersonal world of the infant*. London: Karnac Books Ltd.

Surestart. (2002). *Birth to three matters: a framework to support children in their earliest years*. London: Paul Chapman Publishing.

Trevarthan, C., & Aitken, K. J. (2001). Infant intersubjectivity: Research, theory, and clinical applications. *Journal of Child Psychology and Psychiatry, volume 42*. Cambridge: Cambridge University Press.

United States (US) Department of Health & Human Services. (2011). *Strengthening families and communities:2011 resource guide*. Retrieved on 10 March, 2018, from www.childwelfare.gov/preventing/preventionmonth/guide2011/

Whitebread, D., & Basilio, M. (2011). The emergence and early development of self-regulation in young children. *Profesorado revista de curriculum y formacion* del profeserado. Retrieved on 7 March, 2018, from www.nhs.scot.knowledge.network

Whitters, H. G. (2018). *Family learning to inclusion: Theory, practice, and partnerships.* (pp. 20–23). Abingdon: Routledge.

Wolff, P. H. (1965). The development of attention in young infants. *Annals New York Academy of Sciences, volume 118,* 815–830. Retrieved on 7 March, 2018, from www.nhs.scot.knowledge.network

2 Implementation gap and professional development

This chapter contributes to discussion of links between research and practice by focusing upon policy and theoretical principles. The issues are illustrated to the reader in a context of the outdoor learning environment. The chapter includes a section on professional development.

Policy

One role of research and policy in this field is identification of principles and directives to promote positive outcomes for two generations, mother and child. This is an example of promotion of policy with the greatest impact value: educating one generation in a parenting role in order to have a direct influence upon the next, and potentially subsequent generations. The research team from Harvard University identified that building of carers' skills and promotion of mental and physical health pre-term were core principles in relation to policy-making and parenting programmes (Center on the Developing Child at Harvard University, 2016).

A child's potential for executive functioning is already forming from the moment of conception. There are many facets to the debate on a generational impact upon executive functioning in children. Policy on childcare and education is informed by and informs research from around the world and promotes the significance of creating optimum conditions for growth at every stage of development (Champagne, 2015). An example from the Scottish context is presented by The Children and Young People (Scotland) Act 2014 as a preventative approach to supporting families (Scottish Government, 2014). This model, called Universal Health Visiting Pathway in Scotland Pre-birth to Pre-school, focuses upon strengths and needs in the earliest stages of life (Scottish Government, 2015). The following examples of early interventional strategies are designed to influence mother and baby in the pre-conception period, during gestation and post-birth: promotion of mental wellbeing, a clean environment through minimising pollution, mandatory additions to common staple foods in the form of vitamins/minerals and free supplements for good physical health.

The responsibility and accountability of ensuring that parent and child experience optimum practice resides within each organisation and associated inspectorate. Policy can activate influences that are positioned externally to the expectant mother, but each mother's reaction, and acceptance of intervention, is dependent on her inner working model: genetic make-up, cultural beliefs, personality, emotional wellbeing, and a readiness to learn. My experience in child protection informs a realistic view that vulnerable children are supported by parents who have also experienced adversities in childhood, and continue to be affected through low resilience and negative lifestyles.

Practice

21st century workforce

At times, from a practitioner's stance, the perspective is overwhelming due to the multiple aspects which have to be considered in the care and education of our youngest citizens. You may question the significance of research. You may reflect upon the achievements of previous generations, or even refer to historical examples of influential people, and wonder whether this current increase in our knowledge of neuroscience is necessary for practice.

Practice knowledge

Comprehension can emerge from a knowledge of practice without the deep level of learning which can be derived from theory based upon research findings. Practice knowledge is acquired over time, and it always emerges from the experiential learning opportunities of the worker. This information is interpreted, configured and used for interaction in accordance with the inner working model of each practitioner.

Understanding of practice accumulates and inadvertently forms a personal and professional standard for reference which is pertinent to each employee. Every organisation has a particular culture of practice, and pedagogy evolves from the needs of the service-users, and the expertise, personalities and standards of the service-providers. Financial restrictions in the current recession have led to a trend in organisations only delivering continuous professional development in the format of in-house training sessions. Internal training is a relevant medium for information sharing, and it supports comprehension of local needs; however, it is common for long-standing practitioners in childcare and education to remain in the same employment for lengthy periods, which can restrict and narrow their sources of learning.

Additionally, an implementation gap can occur through unforeseen responses of the service-provider or the service-user. Optimum practice is supported by reference to curricula, guidance frameworks, legislation and the use of cultural sensitivity to respond to specific needs of individuals within a community.

Research knowledge

It is equally important to source deep level learning from beyond the boundaries of a service. Accessing national and international research, reviewing policies and legislation from other countries, rejoicing in similarities and carefully considering differences will lead to a competent, broadly educated workforce. I felt that my practice was transformed through studying research. This type of learning leads to an increase in comprehension which is based upon the rationale provided by theory, and subsequently promotes objectivity and consistency of practice in each workplace, and contributes to disseminating a high standard throughout a nation.

Theoretical principles in practice

Our world is changing. You may say that every corner of the earth is more accessible, you may say that the world is a smaller place or your world is larger, or you may say that communications between continents are faster and easier – whatever your perspective, there is a growing realisation in services throughout the world that children and parents need to be supported to function well, and to perform effectively in a diversity of circumstances in order to benefit self and others. Development towards a sense of the autobiographical self, maintenance of executive functioning and an increase in using this ability within different contexts are regarded as positive outcomes.

Theory deepens our learning, facilitates the transfer of concepts to different contexts and supports consistent implementation of practice. Outdoor Nurseries are the latest pilot projects and focus for early intervention in Scotland. Pilot ventures do impose pressures upon a workplace through expectations of professional achievement, the creation of a universal service template and the uncertainty of securing future funding.

Principles are the strap-lines from theoretical frameworks. These tenets are composed with diligence, and every word entraps wisdom and encourages the reader to seek out links to further and deeper comprehension.

Principles represent findings from research and the few words of knowledge may be the result of many years of collecting and analysing data in the field.

- Principles provide boundaries to learning which support professionals to focus upon a specific topic.
- Principles maintain integrity of knowledge and validity to the rationale of a particular practice approach.
- Principles provide a necessary framework to guide and to lead practice.
- Finally, principles can be used to bridge the implementation gap.

I decided to increase my knowledge through participation in Nurture Training (Bennathan & Boxall, 2013), and the following sections explore the use of Nurture Principles (The Nurture Group Network, 2015) as a theoretical framework for learning in outdoor play.

Principle 1: Children's learning is understood developmentally (The Nurture Group Network, 2015)

The Outdoor Nursery has been utilised by organisations to support school transitions, to nurture a child's readiness to learn and to develop the ability and capacity to be an active participant. The outdoor environment is a medium for learning with a particular focus upon the use of the five senses. There are numerous planned and unplanned opportunities to support children to gain a sense of the physical self within this social context. Additionally, children can link ideas, and eventually concepts, as they plan, implement and reflect, as individuals and by following peer-models. A child's interpretation of the outdoor environment may vary at each session, and reflects his emotional status, maturity, long- or short-term needs, and his understanding of self. A specific outdoor context of play cannot be replicated from one session to another, and there are many implicit and explicit challenges for the professional and child. Beneficial outcomes for mental and physical good health, in addition to social development, have been extensively published (O'Brien & Murray, 2007).

Formative assessment of children's developmental levels is a systematic approach which practitioners use to comprehend each child's interpretation of learning opportunities, and to use personalised responding which supports attainment. The inclusion of children who have additional support needs in mainstream schools has greatly contributed to understanding children's needs, and the complexities of human development. The use of developmental norms provides the practitioner with a means to calibrate the progress of each child objectively, and to influence planning and consistent implementation of curricula within each service, local authority and beyond. Comparison to normative standards also supports the referral process for specialist intervention within an opportune time-frame.

The delivery of curricula within a range of experiences, indoors and outdoors, underpins practice in the child's earliest years. Skills associated with executive functioning, for example, the use of working memory, shifting and self-regulation of behaviour (Diamond, 2013) influence social conduct, and the ability to function effectively in different contexts. Practice has shown me that development of self is dependent on responses to a child's *stage* of learning as opposed to age. It is essential that a foundation for learning is created, re-configured, consolidated and extended in the early stages of childhood through active learning and scaffolding by an attachment figure.

Principle 2: The importance of nurture for the development of wellbeing (The Nurture Group Network, 2015)

It is well known that secure attachment with primary and secondary carers is a key condition of learning in early childhood, and the effect has a life-time value (Bowlby, 1979). Our first relational experiences as children guide us through the creation of relationships with peers, colleagues or partners in adulthood. We remember the positive emotions experienced at the beginning of friendships or partnerships, and the intense happiness and contentment which is gained from a secure attachment relationship with another being. We experience the feeling of invincibility and the positive perception of life's challenges as support and encouragement can easily be accessed, and given freely with reassuring predictability and consistency. We bask in the glory of shared successes which increase ten-fold if acknowledged by a significant other in our lives.

Secure attachment provides a child with a consistent and predictable base to access informational and emotional support during his quest to explore and to seek out understanding of his changing world. Every early years' educator is familiar with the significance of positive relationships within the confines of an organisation; however, delivering a service in a different venue, or transitioning from an internal planned and regulated environment to external play setting, requires this concept of attachment to be re-examined. It is easy for a child to access an attachment figure within a playroom, but there may be physical barriers and greater distances between adults and children in outdoor play areas. A display of positive body language, and verbal reassurance, can promote resilience by offering support without physical proximity.

Why?

Discussion of the processes which occur during a secure attachment relationship respond to the practitioner's need for understanding (Fonagy et al., 2007; Howe, 2011).

- Children are more likely to absorb and respond to knowledge from a secure attachment figure.
- The knowledge may well be culturally applicable and necessary to survival, which presents the rationale for this predisposition in young children, for example, within an outdoor environment.
- The knowledge may respond to a child's personal needs at a point in time.
- Finally, the knowledge may be promoted to the child in a manner or medium which is tailored to his emotions, therefore gaining priority for the child's attention.

Fonagy et al. (2007) indicate that babies and young children will reflect adult interpretation of the world in the early stages of self, and knowledge gains currency which depends on the source. The attachment figure holds the greatest value.

Children are traditionally immersed in the values and attitudes of their birth family which directly influence actions, behaviour and emotions. The rapid increase in childcare and education by services places emphasis on the role and responsibilities of the early years' worker in this area of practice. Social referencing is indefinable, and at times imperceptible, and children can adopt perceptions and attitudes of secondary carers which may conflict with family values. Pedagogy should always promote and uphold each child's rights within the context of family and individually, which include the right to learn and to be protected from harm (Balbernie, 2013).

Principle 3: All behaviour is communication, and Principle 4: Language is a vital means of communication (The Nurture Group Network, 2015)

Semantics and changes in comprehension over time can affect the application of principles. I feel that the descriptor *vital* could be replaced by the term *important* in reference to the use of verbal language in communication. In the earliest years and beyond, the new-born baby, infant and child will use behaviour as representation of his or her emotions, needs, interests and attachment status. The development of verbal language is significant, but any other strategies of communication, formal or informal, should be regarded with equal worth as a child's means of making an impact upon his world. The active promotion of inclusion in the last few years has disseminated a deeper understanding of the importance of noticing and valuing different forms of communication by a child.

Outdoor play areas require different forms of communication to be developed and applied which are relative to the environment, additional support for learning needs and each child's reaction to this context. A child's behaviour may change in the outdoor arena and demonstrate a lower level of functioning in the initial stages of exposure to new experiences. Children often use basic sensory exploration to seek out learning prior to demonstration of current and latent skills.

Observation

Observation of children over time is a key feature of assessment of need (Bomber & Hughes, 2013), regardless of learning environment. Practice has shown me that professional observations have three levels which are accumulative and significant to interpretation of behaviour.

1. Descriptive, the scene unfolds – what do I see?
2. Analytic, the context, internal and external factors are considered – what does it mean?
3. Application, next steps to development – how do I use this information?

Principle 5: The classroom offers a safe base, and Principle 6: The importance of transition in children's lives (The Nurture Group Network, 2015)

Research shows that the optimum learning environment is predictable and consistent (Moran et al., 2004; Siraj-Blatchford et al., 2002), and transitions to unfamiliar venues and changes in circumstances, need to be supported. This process maintains executive functioning and releases transferrable skills.

As professional learners we are aware of the concept of transferrable skill-sets within our continuous professional development framework for registration purposes. We are often guided in this area by flow-charts and indicators. Adapting skills to different contexts is essential for development and attainment of children. Children who exist within a disorganised, chaotic home lifestyle are vigilant, and expect negative reactions from peers, but a transitional medium can be provided by a secure attachment figure.

A therapeutic alliance and strengths-based approach were identified as key factors in motivation and readiness to learn in children (Lewing et al., 2018).

It is easy to ensure and maintain the environmental safety of an outdoor site through policies and procedures and clearly defined areas of responsibility; however, maintaining a secure relationship is equally important. Relationship-based practice supports each child to embrace new situations with positivity, and facilitates learning. Adopting a whole-service approach to nurturing provides a child with holistic intervention which applies to outdoor or indoor learning environments within a community. Weare (2015) indicated the value of communities, and organisations working together to promote emotional and social wellbeing.

Professional reflection

The use of nurture principles as a framework to develop knowledge and understanding of outdoor learning is interesting. Readers may already have a well-established and pertinent theoretical approach to this extension in the environments of learning for young children in the United Kingdom and elsewhere. Consideration of any theory prompts us to reflect, to consider issues at a deeper level of learning, to acquire knowledge based upon research and to use findings in order to gain insight into practice which is applicable to our own role. Subsequently we transfer this increase in comprehension into practical skill in the context of our responsibilities, and review the applicability of this expertise to individual learners in respect of their rights, needs and aspirations.

Theories should be reviewed and revised over time, and education invokes the freedom to make changes which are valid and rational. As soon as a theory is applied there is a potential change to practice which in turn may inform the theoretical framework. Matching theory and practice in order to close the implementation gap is not an exact science, and there cannot be a definitive outcome in the early years of human development. The ever-evolving nature of these processes provides the key to professional development and responsive care by promoting life-long learning for the service-provider, as well as the service-user.

As professionals we continue to be learners who are affected mildly or markedly by the ecological systems which encompass our existence, regardless of age and stage of our career-pathways. Human beings, young or old, are influenced by internal and external factors to development. The Ecological Systems' Theory of Human Development (Bronfenbrenner, 2006) is used to underpin practice – for example, the Scottish National Practice model, Getting It Right for Every Child (Scottish Government, 2008). It is a framework which promotes comprehension of children's lives and supports professionals to identify the optimum entry point for intervention.

Bronfenbrenner's model depicts four concentric circles to represent the sources of influences affecting human development throughout our lifespans. The micro-system encompasses influences nearest to the individual, for example, relationships within the home, service or workplace, and meso-systems create links or bridges between these micro-systems. Influences from the exo-system are indirect, which may encompass factors associated with a community or professional culture, and the macro-system represents the formal effects upon development in a context of legislation, policy or curricula.

During training I became aware of the influences upon my own development in this context of ecological systems. There is pressure from the macro-system in the form of legislation which mandates the necessity for formal registration and continuous training updates. A barrier from the exo-system had originated within funding restrictions, and was alleviated for me by diversion of financial responsibility to the employee. Subsequently, post-training, I gained accountability and responsibility as a messenger with knowledge and understanding who had to create a link, a meso-system between the micro-system of the training course and my workplace in the form of an in-service training session. My course legacy had to be taken further, and my knowledge was embedded within the exo-system of our service by influencing the pedagogy in records and practice. The formal documentation was submitted to the local council and additional funding bodies, set in the macro-system of policy and procedures, and potentially informs other services.

There are additional influences to acquisition of knowledge at a local level in the form of attitudes and perceptions, for example, positivity from a facilitator, the ambience created by the training venue and the personal and professional opinions, values and attitudes from newly acquired colleagues in each break-out group. I was reminded of the impact from group learning upon the individual, and the vulnerability of all human beings in the context of "new learning." Interpretation of course-work by fellow learners can quickly be promoted as desirable standards within a training session. A significant aspect of professional reflection and development is gaining understanding of similarities and differences between the tools that are used in the workplace, and identifying the best approach to support a specific group of service-users.

Self-reflection, and practising with intent and purpose, supports the workforce to apply expertise within multiple contexts for each child, thus extending the learner's experiences and maintaining attachment relationships as a core feature. Additionally, skills can be applied to different age-groups, cultures, countries and within each stage of a vocational career: newly qualified, early stages of experience, maturity of professionalism and the wisdom which emerges in the latter period of a long career.

A deep level of learning is the binding which creates a strong foundation for effective practice and continuous professional development. Today's employment opportunities are far-reaching, and the workforce in the 21st century require flexibility, adaptability and potential to achieve in a diversity of circumstances.

References

Balbernie, R. (2013). *The importance of secure attachment for infant mental health.* Retrieved on 28 March, 2018, from www.researchgate.net/publication/275599605

Bennathan, M., & Boxall, M. (2013). *The Boxall profile handbook (revised).* London: The Nurture Group Network Limited.

Bomber, L. M., & Hughes, D. (2013). *Settling to learn.* London: Worth Publishing.

Bowlby, J. (1979). *The making and breaking of affectional bonds.* (pp. 13, 29–30, 41–45, 84–87, 124–127, 134, 154–155, 165–174, 181–187). Abingdon: Routledge.

Bronfenbrenner, U., & Morris, P. A. (2006). The bioecological model of human development. In W. Damon & R. M. Lerner (Eds.), *Handbook of child psychology, volume 1* (pp. 796–798, 800, 810–815). Hoboken: NJ: Wiley & Sons.

Center on the Developing Child at Harvard University. (2016). *From best practices to breakthrough impacts: A science-based approach to building a more promising future for young children and families.* Retrieved on 1 June, 2016, from www.developingchild.harvard.edu

Champagne, F. A. (2015). Epigenetics of the developing brain. *Zero to Three, Connecting Science, Policy, and Practice, volume 35, number 3*, 2–8. Washington: Zero to Three.

Diamond, A. (2013). Executive functions. *Annual Review of Psychology, volume 64.* Retrieved on 12 June, 2017, from www.annualreviews.org

Fonagy, P., Gergely, G., & Target, M. (2007). The parent-infant dyad and the construction of the subjective self. *Journal of Child Psychology and Psychiatry, volume 48, number 3/4,* 288–328. Oxford: Blackwell Publishing.

Howe, D. (2011). *Attachment across the life course, a brief introduction.* (pp. 32–38, 41–55, 88–112, 157–165, 211, 216). Basingstoke: Palgrave Macmillan.

Lewing, B., Doubell, L., Beevers, T., & Acquah, D. (2018). *Building trusted relationships for vulnerable children and young people with public services.* Retrieved on 1 February, 2018, from www.EIF.org.uk

Moran, P., Ghate, D., & Van der Merwe, A. (2004). *What works in parenting support? A review of the international evidence.* London: Department for Education and Skills.

The Nurture Group Network. (2015). *The theory and practice of nurture groups.* Retrieved on 6 February, 2018, from www.nurturegroups.org

O'Brien, L., & Murray, R. (2007). *Forest school and its impact upon young children: Case studies in Britain.* Retrieved on 28 March, 2018, from www.forestresearch.gov.uk

Scottish Government. (2008). *A guide to getting it right for every child.* (pp. 1–17, 29). Edinburgh: Scottish Government.
Scottish Government. (2014). *Children and young people (Scotland) Act.* Edinburgh: Scottish Government.
Scottish Government. (2015). *Universal health visiting pathway in Scotland, pre-birth to pre-school.* Edinburgh: Scottish Government.
Siraj-Blatchford, I., Sylva, K., Muttock, S., Gilden, R., & Bell, D. (2002). *Researching effective pedagogy in the early years, report number 356.* London: Department for Education and Skills.
Weare, K. (2015). What works in promoting social and emotional well-being and responding to mental health problems in schools? *Partnership for Well-Being and Mental Health in Schools.* Retrieved on 30 June, 2015, from www.ncb.org.uk

3 Intra-personal and inter-personal communication

This chapter explores the link between language and executive functioning. The context includes examples from the pre-verbal developmental stage of childhood, and children who have additional support for learning needs. Communication in the format of verbal language or non-verbal means is integral to provide internal scaffolding of information. Positioning of information for use is significant to actualisation and executive functioning. This increase in knowledge supports the formation of new perceptions or consolidation of prior beliefs and attitude. Sorting our knowledge of the world affects its application in response to our needs and others. Our reciprocal interactions with others are dependent on this internal foundation.

Common ground can be established between academics, practitioners and parents despite the use of different terminology. The phenomenon of private speech, as termed in research, is discussed alongside the use of current practical strategies of tracking, descriptive praise and finally self-affirmation as applied within services, and parenting programmes in the home environment.

EXAMPLE FROM PRACTICE

Intra-personal and inter-personal communication

The lecturer surveyed the class of students and flicked a remote control casually towards the Power Point. The electronic aid gave a quick response, and two concepts shone down upon the learners: intra-personal and inter-personal. Below these words was a common command and powerful teaching strategy – "discuss!" I glanced at my neighbour, and we exchanged rueful smiles. What does this mean?

The context was a university post-graduate class in Glasgow on a Tuesday evening – a twilight session to respond to the needs of full-time working professionals. The class was composed of primary class teachers, headteachers, and me, as an early years' worker.

Returning to formal learning, in order to gain deeper understanding of how children learn, is a challenging and exciting journey. Maturity of experience in adulthood provides a natural foundation for reflection. Maturity supports an adult learner to consider issues objectively, without the distraction of altruism and ill-founded desire to change the world which can temper the learning of youth. Maturity permits the learner to embrace time in the learning process: the confidence to review and to focus upon the details, the ability to question and clarify, and the motivation to return again and again to concepts in order to re-configure the inner working model, and to influence practice in the field.

I used a well-trodden path in my consideration of the two concepts, intra- and inter-personal, and I recalled my early days as an under-graduate. I rapidly became aware of connections stirring in my brain which were prompted by the sensory experience of sitting on the familiar, historical wooden bench, smelling the oak and dust of this ancient learning arena, and listening to the scratching of pencil on paper. My neural networks had been re-activated, dormant for many years but ready to use, and I experienced the palpable sensation of knowledge acquisition, and the joy of understanding.

What does this mean in theory and practice?

Teaching and learning

For us professional educators, it is necessary to comprehend and to respond to the processes of learning, which involves not just sharing specific information or relaying facts but also inducing and reproducing sensory experiences. Learning which invokes acute sensory experience creates "implicit memories." These memories are founded on "emotional reaction," which has a major influence upon a child's investment in learning at a point in time.

"Explicit memories" are based upon the "context," and the significance to a particular learner and his or her circumstances. Relevance will be determined by the developing person, who will subsequently add or detract value from the learning experience. Memories act as prompts which aid each child to access knowledge and understanding throughout life, and impact directly upon executive functioning.

Teaching is an art, and the associated skills can be applied at a basic level in which information is imparted, or a deeper level of comprehension by an educator who nurtures reciprocal relationships between teacher and learner. Every personal glance, nod, gesture or momentary touch which is shared directly with one child, despite a crowded context, reaffirms the dyad for teaching and learning. Communicating with small and large groups is a necessity of practising within an organisation but tiny reminders of the attachment relationship continue to promote the value of knowledge-exchange from professional to child.

The educator imparts enthusiasm, motivation and belief in the learner's ability and capacity to acquire knowledge and understanding. Humans are affected by social referencing, and these features can potentially be adopted by the learner. The educator will teach in a manner which responds to the learner's needs, and emotions, by using personal and professional qualities and strategies – for example:

- High, low, quiet or loud voice,
- Positive open body language,
- Link topic to the environmental context and the context of each learner's circumstances,
- Focus upon creating a learning experience, planned or unplanned, momentarily or over a period of time.

The effective execution of any skill is directly linked to the preparation which involves practising and the ability to look forward; however, learning cannot always be planned, and it is essential to access spontaneous opportunities to support each child's progress. Preparation includes a teacher being ready to identify and respond to learning opportunities. It is important to know yourself in the role of educator by recognising your own skill-set, ability and capacity to teach. Gaining an awareness of your lack of knowledge, your weakest skills and any vulnerabilities in the art of teaching are significant aspects of continuous professional development in the journey of education.

It is essential to interpret and respond to the context. This base of information will enable an educator to nurture a readiness to learn, and to support the developing person to embrace knowledge from a perspective of mental, physical and social wellbeing. Scaffolding by a responsive attachment figure is a key strategy of effective teaching, which results in the child using experiential learning to explore teleological agency and to make an impact upon the learning environment.

Teaching encompasses many processes at different levels. It involves passing the baton of knowledge to another person and presenting a choice of pathways to support comprehension. The infant or child, who operates in a context of secure attachment, will make a personal choice of pathway in relation to learning style, short- or long-term needs, emotions and established or potential neural connections. The choice will also be influenced by guidance from an educator which may be explicit and instructional or implicit relative to the social and cultural context.

The inner working model influences all learning processes. Each learner will apply understanding by using a different skill-set. The executive functioning of every child is unique, and this operational ability is an indicator of the quality of educational environment.

Learning processes

My personal learning memories were activated as I sat in the university lecture theatre every Tuesday evening. Over the past five hundred years there have been countless students seated on the same polished oak benches, poised in anticipation, and inclined towards the educator as learning was sought. Humans do not change a great deal over the centuries, but our understanding of teaching and learning in a context of neuroscience has increased significantly.

For many years it has been recognised that monkeys have a similar approach to learning as human beings, which relates to a group social system. Survival of primates is dependent on the ability to observe, to interpret, to comprehend and to respond to the actions of others in order to benefit oneself and the familial group. Researchers, practitioners and parents are conversant with an infant or child's potential for learning through imitation, and the next section reviews research in this field. The research will be linked to practice in the context of additional support for learning needs through examples.

Mirror neurons

Rizzolatti and Craighero (2004) conducted research on learning through imitation. The research findings indicated a recordable reaction in the brain of monkeys following the performance of an action. This related to "visuo-motor neurons" which were activated in the brain during execution of fine and gross motor skills. The same reaction was recorded in monkeys who "observed" another monkey performing a physical action. Initial mirroring takes place between a mother and baby monkey which derives from a need for safety. This skill is gradually replaced by copying, which means that the baby monkey can reproduce movements within and out-with the initial learning context.

Activation of mirror neurons was presented by these authors as a basis for understanding the actions of others, and the terms strictly or broadly congruent were applied to describe associated reactions (Rizzolatti & Craighero, 2004).

- "Strictly congruent" – initial "mirroring" of actions in which the monkey reflects the motor skill of another monkey by reproducing the same movements.
- "Broadly congruent" – this term relates to "copying" actions. The monkey will observe and remember the motor skills of another monkey, and reproduce a similar, but not identical action, in the same context or another context.

Understanding the actions of others

The mirror neuron system also exists in human beings; however an inhibitory mechanism has been identified in the human spinal cord which can be voluntarily activated to stop execution of a skill (Rizzolatti & Craighero, 2004). This specialism allows the human being to respond to different cultural contexts, social rules and expectations. Lave and Wenger (1991) use the term "legitimate peripheral participation," which refers to the use of local knowledge. Local or cultural knowledge supports an individual to operate effectively within a micro-system or community.

The skill of copying is a necessary stage in the achievement of teleological agency, and the ability facilitates the use of this common, and highly significant source of learning for the developing human being. Mastering the skill of copying entails several stages which the infant has to accomplish:

- "Mirroring" requires the infant to observe another person. Observation can only be an effective source of learning if the baby/child has the appropriately balanced emotional and physical status for this medium to be used. For example, a baby who is crying for food will not be able to learn by observing external stimulus because she is focused upon her internal need.
- A baby who is motivated, and remains in a stable emotional state, will replicate the initial observation. The motor cortex of his brain will experience neuron activity during observation, and links are made to motor movement.
- Over time the infant will reproduce the movement from memory, in the appropriate context and without requiring a visual prompt from an adult.
- Primary carers will inevitably, and unknowingly, extend the baby's learning by linking the baby's sense of self to actions, words and meaning. For example, "You are putting out your tongue. You are telling me that you are hungry."

EXAMPLE FROM PRACTICE

Daily routines and the sense of self: copying

Mercy skipped towards the sink in her nursery wash-room. Life is good when you are four years old, and mandatory hygiene routines present exciting, challenging and achievable goals for development. She surveyed the choices of soap. Workplaces often insert hand soap-dispensers onto the wall above a sink, part of a contracted package by firms approved by the local authority; however, in today's world many children present with allergies or potential local irritations to products which are deemed to be universally non-allergenic. This nursery does have a blue and white wall dispenser. It is easy to use, and the quick release of foam gives sensory satisfaction to young children.

I notice that many children who have autistic spectrum disorder do not like sensory stimulus which is unpredictable. The foam soap is a prime example of a substance which has been manufactured well for an outcome but the spreading of silky foam across little children's fingers, and their inability to remove it quickly, can create a barrier in the wash-room area.

Mercy has spotted a supplementary container of liquid new-born baby soap which can be used for any child who actively rejects the foam cleanser. This four year old girl steps to one side and watches a peer pushing on the soap lever – "observing an action." She has chosen to wait for the baby soap, and looks closely at the stereo-typical picture which adorns the side of the bottle – a smiling blond baby in the arms of her coiffured mother who has rosy cheeks.

Mercy's friend Lily is using one hand to press hard on the lever, and she looks expectantly for the pink trail of soap. The container slides and immediately falls onto the floor. The manufacturing of this type of children's soap is also very effective as a valve ensures that the baby soap does not leak onto the floor-tiles. Every early years' worker rapidly acquires a bank of invaluable information and expertise on children's products.

Mercy quickly retrieves the soap from the floor, and she takes charge of the situation. Mercy holds the soap dispenser horizontally against her jumper, competently presses the lever, and gains a little portion of the cleansing substance – "identifying and achieving a goal." This little four year girl has observed the execution of skill by a peer, and adapts this knowledge to improve the route to goal-achievement – "completion of a task more effectively."

Lily watches and reproduces the actions of her friend. Independently both girls have attempted this task, and independently these young learners have copied each other, and developed their personal skills and executive *functioning* – *"a cooperative venture which requires the ability and capacity to copy, and motivation to achieve a goal."*

What does this mean in theory and practice?

The research of Rizzolatti and Craighero (2004) indicated two different behaviours in humans which can develop from learning through imitation.

1 Following observation, a motor pattern can be developed which supports completion of the task more effectively.
2 A motor pattern can be developed which is applied to achieve a specific goal. This skill involves identification of a goal, and identification of the relevant motor pattern from memory.

A third behaviour which is observable in practice is the use of a motor pattern for a task which is unrelated to the observed task; in other words, the human is applying a skill to a different context = "transferrable skill." This aptitude involves the ability to extrapolate current knowledge, and apply within a new context for the first time. Learners who are able to transfer skills place importance upon the processes in addition to a potential goal. Early years' workers would recognise this area of learning as problem-solving, and imaginative play. In recent years early years' approaches to education have focused upon self-appointed goals in children's play as opposed to goal-setting by professionals. This pedagogy encourages a young learner to focus upon the processes, and achievement of a goal is relative to each child's ability and capacity.

Hand over hand teaching

Children may not have the ability to copy. Research indicates a potential link to immaturity in development of the visuo-motor cortex (Vivanti & Rogers, 2014). This characteristic has been observed in some children who have autistic spectrum disorder. Hand over hand methods of teaching have been implemented for many years to support children who cannot learn through observation and reproduction of actions. Initially a practitioner sits behind a child on the floor. The learning arena can be compartmentalised and present optimum value by minimising distraction from peers or external noises. Sitting behind a child on floor level can create a small area of learning which supports the young learner to focus upon an activity situated close to him, in the space between his hands and feet. An expected outcome is the child's increasing awareness of his personal tools which can be used to explore the proximal environment: development of the physical sense of self.

Safe practice

Additionally, practice requires early years' workers to ensure that the learning environment is safe for child and adult, and to reduce the effect of negative reactions from the child. Every practitioner will have experience of children lunging unexpectedly to one side or the other within a dyad, or head-butting an adult as a reaction to a transition. Interventions at floor level maintain safety of child and adult, and provide both parties with an opportunity to quickly move away from the situation if required. I have always found that positive responses in the safe-guarding of child and adult can be identified for any challenging behaviours through careful planning. It is essential that all practitioners feel supported and protected in this area of work, and parents feel competent, safe and valued in their parenting roles.

Promoting understanding of physical self

The adult will enclose the child's right or left hand in order to use hand over hand directed learning. Young children may not have identified or indicated a hand of preference. This circumstance is particularly relevant to children with an immature sense of physical self, and opportunities for equal use of right and left should be presented. The adult will support the child to touch, and eventually to interact with the object. Actions required should be simple and short with an obvious outcome. The use of two hands is complex, and should be introduced at a later stage of development.

Patterns will be established in the child's neural network through the physical sensations which she experiences, and the visual action and reaction which she observes as supplementary to the sensory acquisition of knowledge. Positive emotions will reinforce her desire for repetition, and seeking out understanding. The adult will gradually move her hand towards the child's wrist so that he can view his own hand; however the adult should continue to facilitate the child's use of his fine motor skills through contact. Eventually the adult can tap the child's hand then tap the object as prompts to replace the hand over hand method. There is an interim stage in which some children will access the adult's hand and use it as a tool to interact with the activity.

Children may well demonstrate reluctance to participate in this new experience but using simple activities, and following through a plan from beginning to end within a few seconds, can capture the child's interest and motivation to remain in this learning dyad. Practice should always capitalise upon a child's favourite activities at a particular point in time. This strategy increases the child's involvement and wellbeing, and also transfers power to the child in the process of gaining intentional mental agency.

Developing understanding of physical self

A developmental stage is the practitioner sitting "in front" of the child, within a direct line of eye contact and tapping the child's hand and object to prompt a motor action. Over time the practitioner will tap the child's hand and point to the object, and eventually prompt through pointing rather than tactility. Words may replace visual pointing as appropriate to the child's ability and capacity. Patterns of visual to motor sequences can be supported in this way, and the child will extend his learning over time by referring to his own established patterns of interaction within an environment. The inner working model is developed and re-configured as learning progresses, based upon the child's "own" experiences as opposed to observation of others.

Sitting in front of a child presents optimum positioning for mirroring and subsequently copying. This provides a foundation for learning which can be extended through the creation of a reciprocal relationship in which eye contact, body language, verbal or sign-language are key prompts for encouraging patterns of play – predicting and responding, eventually turn-taking, and the early stages of self-control as a prelude to self-regulation. Face to face interaction presents a myriad of opportunities for learning and developing.

Scaffolding in play

A child who is unable to observe and copy, and who is not supported through hand over hand teaching may develop repetitive patterns of play. These patterns have formed through the child's independent exploration, and she may be unable to use imagination or extrapolation to further her development. Practitioners comment that some children appear to learn in a random manner, by trial and error or spontaneous occurrences. Learning for any child, regardless of additional support for learning needs, can occur through unplanned circumstances. For example, if a ring is dropped by chance upon a stacking stick then this can create a pattern of play if the child is supported to reproduce the event. Scaffolding in play by a familiar attachment figure is a key aspect of implementation of curricula in early years' services. Research has identified this practice approach as effective to supporting a child to extend her knowledge and understanding (Siraj-Blatchford et al., 2002).

Motor patterns can be developed by introducing objects which require similar skills – for example, different types of stacking toys, and threading large then small beads. Full-length and hand-held mirrors which can be accessed throughout play are essential to support a child's representation of himself. A practitioner can gain great insight into a child's sense of himself by observing the child's use of a mirror in play.

EXAMPLE FROM PRACTICE

Two and a half year old Yacoub is developmentally delayed and awaiting assessment for autistic spectrum disorder. Yacoub runs up and down in the nursery playroom between the frieze-covered wall and the large sunny window. The little boy follows the same path, back and forward, and I observe Yacoub running on tip-toes and flapping his hands. The environmental features provide a visual and physical reminder to the child to stop, and to turn around – "Yacoub regulates his physical self." Steps to development have value for each child on an individual basis. Inclusion of all children in mainstream services can result in parents comparing their child to others, and I make sure that Yacoub's achievement is recorded, and described with passion and enthusiasm to his primary carers.

I take up my position against one wall, and grasp Yacoub's two hands as he runs forward. I use his name as we hold hands, and I present myself as the focus for Yacoub's world. I walk backwards as I lead this young learner towards a pre-set activity. He is reluctant and unwilling. Yacoub tightens his grip on my hands then tries to pull away – a common tactic used by all children as adult-led boundaries and decision-making are rejected. Over time every child will learn to apply this strategy: demonstration of early stage teleological agency, action and reaction to achieve a goal.

Leading a child by two hands, and using rhythmical and consistent step patterns will create a small, personalised medium for transition. Body language can be used to change Yacoub's internal focus to consideration of an interactive world outside his mind. It is challenging for this boy as he is being asked to change position, to change an established pattern of running, to accept a different environment and to operate within an undefined social boundary.

I sit behind Yacoub on the red nursery carpet. I have placed a dark green mat under a stacking stick and positioned three rubber discs on one side. Traditionally early years' services furnish rooms in bright colours although we would probably all agree that pastel shades induce a relaxed atmosphere. Over time, there has been more emphasis on the ambience for learning which can be created by furnishings and colours, and gradually services are replacing vibrant primary colours with mute shades to minimise the distraction from background stimuli. An overuse of background environmental space as a secondary source of learning materials has been identified in nursery and primary schools. Educational prompts which are portrayed on every surface and wall can divert a child's attention from materials within his proximal environment. These circumstances are particularly relevant to children with additional support for learning needs.

A few moments later and Yacoub is fixated upon the activity. I sense a stillness spreading throughout his body as hand over hand we lift a disc, feel the top of our stacking ring and let go – a resounding clatter on the wooden base confirms to Yacoub and myself that the goal is achieved: understanding enriches this little boy's knowledge.

What does this mean in theory and practice?

There is always a rationale for every waiting list in services. As a young early years' worker I experienced frustration as I consoled parents regarding long waiting times; however, over the years I have appreciated that children's development takes place within a family and community context, 24 hours a day, seven days a week, throughout every year of childhood.

Understanding and optimum application of support mechanisms have changed in recent times. A significant aspect, and responsibility of the clinical expert, is to upskill primary and secondary carers in order that a child is immersed within learning environments during every moment of the earliest years, and beyond. Weekly or monthly clinic-based intervention is useful, but strategies have the greatest effect if implemented regularly and consistently within a family and community culture. It is important that parents and practitioners recognise their areas of expertise but also embrace knowledge and understanding which is shared from integrated agencies. Current practice involves initial assessment and prioritisation of support which responds to the child's stage of development. Today's support mechanisms are integrated by professionals and parents, and promote personalised responsive care in real-life circumstances.

The research of Vivanti and Rogers (2014) presents three aspects of social learning which have particular significance in responding to the needs of children with autistic spectrum disorder: copying, motivation and application. These authors also refer to the normative developmental processes which occur in the earliest days, months and years of life, and incur the skills of copying and transferring knowledge and understanding to different contexts. The research findings indicated that motivation to learn is gained from social feedback in the form of recognition of accomplishment of personal goals, and achieving outcomes which are set by others.

Learning from an attachment figure has the greatest value due to emotional investment in this significant relationship. Children who have autistic spectrum disorder do not seek this reward; therefore motivation to participate in social learning is diminished. Opportunities to access social interaction are not readily accessed by the child, which reduces the ability and capacity to operate effectively within different social contexts.

Practice strategies which are used in stimulation of young infants are often used with children who have autistic spectrum disorder, for example, a reciprocal relationship, babbling and singing, repetition of actions and routines, mirroring and copying and establishing consistent patterns within daily living.

Primates

Humans have evolved a complex communication system which contains many predictable and transferrable patterns throughout the world within different languages but also refinements which are relevant to a specific region. It is useful to refer to a simple system in order to understand the communication needs of children, and the link to a sense of self.

Monkeys are primates who are associated with the human species. Primates will often react to threat by maintaining group safety in addition to self-protection. Monkeys use a high-pitched scream to communicate a source of danger to their troop but also to access support in responding to this area of immediate need. The monkey is using sound as a link to his own motor reaction, and also using sound as a communication technique to direct the actions of others.

A high-pitched sound is easier to distinguish above the daily noises which occur within a natural habitat. A scream involves a short exhale of breath which does not detract from the energy required to evade an adversary. Personal survival and protection of young is paramount. Over time the danger sound becomes inextricably linked to potential threat, and monkeys in a troop will use and react to the sound in a consistent manner, without the necessity of visual mirroring. A communication strategy has evolved which is based upon visuo-motor neurons.

Recent research by Bob Yirka (2015) has identified that a species of monkey which lives on the Ivory Coast, Diana monkeys, will react appropriately to alarm calls which are specifically used by a neighbouring species, Campbell monkeys. The Diana monkeys have developed the ability to differentiate between calls which relate to different types of danger in the vicinity, and react accordingly. The findings indicated that the alarm calls differed in relation to the addition or elimination of a suffix.

It seems that the rationale of a communication system is a response to personal need, survival and relationships. We are always learning from research, and these findings present fascinating insight into the evolving development of communication by this group of primates who are so closely related to human beings.

EXAMPLE FROM PRACTICE

Human beings are regarded as being the only known species with a complex and complete language system; however humans use a similar alert system to other primates. A high-pitched scream will be used by male or female as a response to a recognisable or unknown source of danger. Children will often scream in a context of play during imaginary games which represent danger in real life. Imaginary play provides opportunities to practice life-skills and/or to gain understanding of past events. Humans will scream even in situations of isolation from other beings. This communication strategy is a direct signal for help but also warns an adversary that support has been summoned.

Being safe continues to be a dominant aspect of our lives in the 21st century. For example, common colloquial terms which are used in daily partings reflect the importance of this issue, "Watch yourself," "You take care," "You be safe," or "Call if you need me." The use of particular communication phrases are often relevant to a specific region, and emphasise relationships, roles, responsibilities and expectations.

Communication does not simply occur during moments of danger for monkeys and other primates. It is also used to publicise a need, for the instinctive desire for a relationship and companionship within a social group.

Motor action and language

Parents

Iverson (2010) highlights the increase in social opportunities and, consequently, interactions which coincide with an infant's development of motor skills during the first two years of life. Sitting independently, rolling over, crawling and walking are proudly cited by all parents as recognisable and formally recorded milestones in childhood. Parents demonstrate a sense of family achievement as they share details of their child's prowess with practitioners in services.

Alternatively, a feeling of parental failure can emerge from multiple assessments to determine a diagnosis of additional support for learning needs. Multi-disciplinary professionals will frequently, and unintentionally, seek the same information from parents regarding motor milestones. Implicit value is placed upon motor achievement which a parent may interpret as a benchmark for attainment throughout childhood.

Professional recording of this information is often completed in front of parents who sit in a state of anxiety, and may question their capacity to fulfil roles as competent educators and carers of their young. Thirty years ago, at the beginning of my career, professionals would seek information from parents and record in descriptive detail before transferring to the diagnostic record sheets. This definitive information was confidential from parents' view until interpretation and understanding could be shared in an appropriate and supportive context. Times have changed, and pressure upon the professional to process service-users quickly and competently is high. Service-users expect timely feedback. Collating achievement as qualitative data has given way to assessment records which are completed at the first point of contact with primary carers.

Tools have changed too: paper and pencil to pens and checklists or electronic recording. It can be stressful for parents to sit across from a professional in a clinic consultation room, to be faced with the back view of a laptop lid, and to listen and attempt to interpret the rapid or hesitant clicks on the keyboard as a professional represents their child on e-forms.

In today's society parents of children who have learning needs often describe a life-changing traumatic event as a paediatric specialist completing a check-list headed "normative development." The format of these records has changed through time to represent ability, inability and disability: inserting a tick or a cross, or writing "note below – not yet achieved," or perhaps fully or partially shading a representative skill-box which is relative to generic norms.

Over the years I have accompanied many families to parent-specialist information sharing meetings, clinical observations and emotive feedback sessions. It is humbling to observe human resilience. A silence can descend upon the professional-parent dyad despite the back-drop of inner city noise: the raucous clatter of magpies, refuse collectors uploading and frequent sirens. The professional worker in this emotive context resorts to a strategy gained from training, "when delivering diagnostic feedback allow the parent emotional space."

I admire the stoicism of parents as they receive diagnostic information in a clinical setting, and I identify with the well-used phrase which we all apply to protect our emotion: "I knew anyway." However resilience can be short-term, and applicable within a particular context. On a practical level my work has given me knowledge of the locations of paediatric peripatetic services, and the local adjoining coffee-shops where distressed parents attempt to assimilate the diagnostic information on their most valuable asset – a child.

A diagnosis should encompass a plan for care and education, and maintain the joy of parenthood for every family regardless of identified needs. Active parenting is laced with hope for each child's achievement, hope for family pride and hope that this generation will have aspirations which can be met, and impact upon the world.

Children

Babbling, in the form of repetitive sounds which accompany an infant's exploration of the world, represents a foundation in the ever evolving partnership between overt sound and motor action. The research by Iverson (2010) is significant for practitioners and parents in the early years and gives deeper insight into the use of singing, clapping, marching and the instinctive application of repetitive action and sound during the earliest years. Infants gain practice in gross motor skills and regulation of these actions which creates a template for vocalisation. Speech encompasses repetition, order, rules and emotion. Sitting in an upright position and walking or running are complementary skills to growth and development of lung capacity and vocal tract.

Findings do not imply that motor development is necessary for language development, or that the pace of achieving motor milestones is commensurate with stages of language acquisition. The research concludes by explaining that language can also be learned in contexts outside the domain of normative motor skills (Iverson, 2010). For example, babies who have deaf parents use babbling, and can be supported to develop language through signing by their parents, in addition to exposure to verbal communication.

Attachment figure

An attachment figure is essential in childhood, and practitioners are adept at identifying children who have benefited from parental input, or demonstrate a lack of experience in social interaction, communication and opportunities for physical development. Curricula and practice models throughout the world support daily professional-child interactions through promotion of holistic development and understanding of the ecological systems which affect human beings (Bronfenbrenner, 1979). Attachment figures can be parents or extended family, professionals, peers or siblings, and the primary principle is consistent, predictable and responsive care. Current practice nurtures a child's strengths in order to provide a focus for leading learning. Accessing personal strengths also contributes to the child's inner working model as a framework which guides holistic development during formative years.

The years from birth to five can be turbulent but rewarding for child and parent. Norms provide necessary guidance but internal and external adversities, and personality and interests, can affect the child's progress along the stereotypical linear path of normative development. Every early years' worker acquires inter-personal skill in explaining to concerned primary carers that children are individuals, and developmental progress can be recognised and celebrated in many different guises.

What does this mean in theory and practice?

An integral feature of language development is the presence and active support of an attachment figure (Bowlby, 1979). The effect of a secure attachment relationship is often described and recognised by outcomes relating to a child's involvement, wellbeing and executive functioning; however, there is also an ethereal undefinable aspect of this relationship which is based on sensitive and empathic responding to a child's emotions in addition to care of needs. The effect of adversities can be reduced by consistent and predictable responsive care, and ultimately a child's outlook on life can be transformed in a moment by the presence of his or her appointed attachment figure.

Intra-personal communication

Our understanding of the rationale and application of self-directed language has changed during the last hundred years. In the early 1900s Piaget (2001) referred to this phenomenon as "ego-centric speech," and he dismissed any relevance to development of cognitive processes in humans. Some years later Vygotsky critiqued this belief, and placed great emphasis on the use of self-talking to the formation of higher psychological functions (Vygotsky, 1986). This ability distinguishes human primates from animals.

Vygotsky and internalisation of language

Lev Vygotsky (1986) was a researcher whose work continues to be highly influential to our understanding of language and development. He has left a legacy of knowledge and understanding in the field of human development which continues to be reviewed, debated and applied to practice in the 21st century.

Vygotsky was born in Belorussia in 1896, and died in his prime in 1934. He achieved the first of many academic publications at the age of 18 years. As a young boy, Vygotsky had private tutoring as his early experience of education, and in his late teens this avid learner enrolled at the Medical School of Moscow University; however within a few weeks of the first semester the young student had recognised his passion for the written and spoken word, and he transferred to law school. An integral decision to Vygotsky's career was the completion of a history and philosophy degree alongside law, and he demonstrated an increasing desire to study communication, and the links between thought and speech. At the beginning of the 1920s Vygotsky lectured in psychology to student teachers, and throughout this period he developed a life-long interest in education in the field of additional support for learning needs.

This researcher described language, and internalisation, as a means to control thoughts and behaviour which is specific to human primates. Vygotsky (1978) promoted the significance of language acquisition to the human being by identifying this form of communication as a key aspect of developmental change. Language is used to achieve a higher level of functioning which encompasses motivation and intention – these features are absent in the ape-family.

Vygotsky's "law of double formation" is still used to promote understanding of intra-personal and inter-personal processes in the context of language use. Double formation refers to two levels of higher psychological functions:

1   Intra-personal = the function of language is supporting internal cognitive thinking during preparation for executive functioning.
2   Inter-personal = the function of language is social interaction with others in which knowledge, understanding and emotions can be shared, and support sought as appropriate.

Terms may vary in research, and Rodriguez and Palacios (2007) use the terms "intra-mental" and "inter-mental levels" of communication to express this phenomenon.

Language function

Research by Winsler et al. (2000) describes language competence as an indicator of normal and atypical behavioural development. It is widely believed that language has three functions in the earliest years of childhood. Language supports a child:

1   To process thoughts
    The term "internalization" is often used to denote this process of sorting knowledge and understanding in order that executive functioning can occur. Private speech or overt speech to oneself is regarded as an indicator that a child is processing his thoughts through internalisation, which informs the inner working model (Bowlby, 1979). The use of private speech in the early years has been found to follow a particular developmental pathway in the use of unrelated or related overt speech with a particular task, and overt or partial speech to self-regulate (Winsler et al., 2000).
2   To communicate with others
    Speech can be used to gain support from others to complete a task. This request may be self-limiting, for example, "Show me," or a child may describe his plan to the adult and ask for specific support. Practice

shows that scaffolding and reciprocal interactions between child and adult incorporate examples of inter-personal and intra-personal communication. Words can confer emotion, intellectual capacity and desire to another person.

3   To self-regulate behaviour.

Vygotsky (1978) distinguished between two types of memory. "Natural memory" is created by the influence of stimulus which is external to the child, and links to the formation of perceptions. The second type of memory "incorporates signs" which are self-generated. These signs are applied by individuals as memory prompts which link to social and cultural influences, and expectations. Current practice terms are "explicit" and "implicit" memories.

EXAMPLES FROM PRACTICE

1   The use of overt speech which does not relate to the task being performed.

Nine month old Ruby babbles as she sits confidently in a bath. Ruby's mother smiles in delight as her young daughter says, "Mu, mu, mu, mum," and uses an open hand to make an impact upon the warm, bubbled water.

2   The use of overt speech which is directly relevant to the immediate task.

Three year old Alison sits on a small orange bean-bag. Her legs are outstretched to balance a large baby doll and assorted collection of clothing. Alison picks up a yellow tee-shirt which is adorned with a sun-flower, and she says, "Now, I'll just put this on my doll to keep her warm."

3   The use of overt speech which is directly relevant and supports the child to self-regulate his behaviour during task implementation.

Four year old Yang kneels on the floor, and surveys his play-scene. A moment before the little boy had opened a stacking doll, and each different-sized doll-piece lay in waiting. Yang makes a move. He attempts to fit a large head with a wooden doll's body which is slightly smaller. The red smiling doll's head envelops the body. Yang shakes his head affirmatively and proclaims, "Not that one!" Two quick movements and the pieces are returned to the starting point.

4   The use of overt speech which is directly relevant, and partially internalised; for example, the child may whisper or use parts of a sentence overtly.

Arusha is a petite four year old. She is sitting on a nursery chair which is pulled neatly into the table – a skill which Arusha has recently mastered, and practises often during her exploits. Arusha is observed tracking her own fine motor skills as she threads little wooden beads onto a wand. The learner focuses and states, "Through the hole," then she nods and confirms goal achievement. A moment later, and a couple of nods from Arusha during execution of her skills, and a second bead has reached its destination. The little girl whispers, "I did it!"

What does this mean in theory and practice?

Each example demonstrates that the child is linking motor action and verbal expression or vocalisation. It is interesting to read Vygotsky's interpretation of communication without language as he applies the descriptor "spread of affect" which refers to the emotional processes and impact (Vygotsky, 1986). A primitive communication system is based upon demonstration, and transference of emotion between members of a species which may be followed by motor action. For example, a sea-gull will communicate fear to a family group through commencing flight in response to perceived danger. The flock will invariably follow. This action could be developed through mirroring, copying and application within different contexts.

Vygotsky (1978) felt that maturation was a secondary aspect of human development, and he placed emphasis on accumulation of learning; however it may be that maturation is integral to achievement of higher levels of functioning. Valid interpretation of receptive language requires prior knowledge of word meaning, an awareness of cultural context, and understanding of another's emotion and motivation. Repetition, patterning and opportunities occur externally and internally over time as humans transcend from childhood into adulthood. Development and maturation are inseparable. Children's development is never static regardless of the complexity of any additional support for learning needs. This topic is further discussed in the next chapter, "Attainment and Executive Functioning."

Internalisation of language

Communication in the earliest days of childhood is based upon a baby's expression of emotion which is followed by an adult responding. A young baby communicates a need by crying but does not initially identify the source of need or direct his plea for assistance to a particular person. After a few weeks of parenting or perhaps sooner, most mothers and fathers can accurately identify needs which are associated with different types of crying. A baby will learn to direct his cry to a particular person, namely an attachment figure. Each cry is specific to a need, and context, and it represents the emergence of a communication system between primary carer and infant.

Vygotsky (1986) published a book, *Thought and Language*, in 1934 in which he applied the term, "inner speech" to denote internalisation of language as integral to organisation of cognitive processes. He regarded language as units of meaning which can be used for social interaction, and contain a combination of thoughts and speech.

Interesting points for practice were raised in a research study conducted by Winsler et al. (2000). Findings indicated that there is an increase in the use of private speech by children within settings in which the pedagogy emphasises self-regulation of behaviour. Also, there is a correlation in the frequency and content of overt private speech, and opportunities for social interactions with adults. The children who had behavioural issues applied self-talk equally with participants in the norm grouping of this research, and the self-talk was synchronised with motor actions for both groups.

It is clear that private speech supports children to self-regulate their behaviour, and this strategy has always been encouraged within practice; however application of knowledge, without comprehension by the practitioner, is weak and can result in inconsistency and lack of purpose and regulation. Access to research on this topic and promotion within training courses have had a positive influence upon practice, and provided rationale for current child-led pedagogy in the United Kingdom and around the world. Active learning through self-directed play in the presence of an attachment figure is currently being promoted in the first year of primary schools, in addition to nurseries. Sensitive responding to each child's needs is a significant principle in practice today which contributes to executive functioning (Whitebread & Basilio, 2011).

Informal approaches incur direct questions to a child to prompt overt tracking of his play and the practitioner role-modelling the child's actions through descriptive story-telling as the play unfolds. Formal intervention (Bratton et al., 2006) is also used to support children to develop a sense of the autobiographical self, and increase their involvement and wellbeing within a learning environment. The child is prompted to use self-talk by a facilitator tracking his movements during individual half-hour therapeutic sessions (Whitters, 2018). Parenting programmes encourage primary carers to value language as a medium to promote development, and to increase the child's understanding of herself – for example, the use of descriptive praise (Sanders, 1999).

Private gestures

Adults instinctively use gestures in pre-language communication with children. The most popular television programmes for the youngest children involve characters who use signs to represent words, gestures to represent emotion and simple words to convey a message.

Rodriguez and Palacios (2007) researched a potential link between an infant's use of gestures and self-regulation. Findings indicated that private gestures support reflection, which in turn facilitates the emergence of skills associated with self-regulation. Self-regulation involves task-shifting, and the child's tracking of his movements guide his skill performance in real time, and creates patterns in his neural networks which represent the execution of thought into motor action. Partial use of speech indicates internalisation of thoughts and ideas which inform the child's inner working model. An interim stage is often apparent in practice which involves a child using a gesture to him or herself in place of overt speech as described in the examples of four year old Yang and Arusha.

EXAMPLE FROM PRACTICE: FIVE MONTHS OLD

Five month old Paulo sits in a high chair. The chair is modern, made of smooth pale pine-wood and unadorned with decoration. Manufacturers are following nursery good practice guidelines by supporting young children to focus upon self-help skills without the distraction of nursery characters walking and dancing across a high chair. Paulo's feeding experience has been gained over countless practice sessions during his short life. The little hungry boy puts his head to one side as his mother clips the safety harness – always two clicks. He prepares himself for the next step as she automatically runs a finger around his tummy to ensure that the harness is not too tight. Paulo relaxes and waits in anticipation. His world is organised and predictable.

The young mother stretches up high upon her tip-toes in order to retrieve the tin of baby milk powder. She switches on the shiny metal kettle and it hums into action. The baby boy nods and sways back and forward in his chair, feeling the restriction of his harness as he watches and listens to his mother counting out several spoons of milk powder: one and two and three and four and five and six and seven then add to the water, shake the bottle, check the temperature. Paulo's mother vocalises her movements and shares this experience with her son.

She is maintaining his interest, creating a focus to his learning and increasing his patience and ability to wait expectantly. This mother is not aware that her links between actions and language are beginning to create an essential base of knowledge in the baby's brain through patterns forming in his neural networks – the early stages of literacy, numeracy, science, social rules, self-regulation and affirmation of their secure attachment relationship.

EXAMPLE FROM PRACTICE: TWO YEARS OLD

Amber is two years old. She is an avid problem-solver, and seeks out challenges. The little girl sits under an art table in nursery. The table has been draped with bubble-wrap for sensory painting, and Amber has accessed the spot as a reclusion for exploration of her new activity. A wooden box with a sliding lid is placed in centre stage under the table, and multiple tiny broken pieces of green and yellow chalk and several chunky shapes are tucked under Amber's legs – well hidden from her peers – Amber has a plan.

The sliding lid on the box is already open by a tiny margin which allows this explorer to push the pieces of chalk inside. One, two and three, shake the box, confirm the location. Amber can be observed making small movements with her lips as she concentrates on the task, creating an aperture which resembles the small opening in the lid of her wooden box. Amber lifts her legs up high like a ballerina, and she checks for any stray chalk.

Stage two has been reached. The problem is apparent – how can the lid be opened further to deposit the shapes? Amber taps and shakes and bangs the box upon the floor. She whispers, "Open, open, open!" Her lips make tiny movements. An observant practitioner gives advice from the other side of the bubble-wrap curtains, "Amber pull the lid – two hands!"

The two year old inserts both hands into the tiny aperture, and opens her mouth wide as she pulls determinedly, again and again. Lid open, shapes away and goal achieved. Amber rejects the box quickly and joins her peers. Goal achievement for our youngest children usually represents an immediate end to the activity. It is only as children mature through childhood that they view, and review their achievement, and seek to share the success with others.

What does this mean in theory and practice?

Young babies will particularly invest in learning which responds to imminent need for example, hunger or thirst. In the weeks after birth a baby will quickly associate adult-initiated signs and environmental prompts with the meeting of her needs – preparation for breast-feeding, a mother taking a tin of milk out of a cupboard, the familiar clatter on the work-top, and the ping of a kettle as hot water comes to boiling point. The baby will develop the earliest stages of temporal understanding. Her expectation of receiving her warm milk will relate to observation of these signs, which are preludes to the main event.

Effective operational capacity relates to activation of tried and tested patterns of functioning in human beings. Preparation in the form of routines promotes self-regulation during the main task. Humans do not like surprises, particularly in relation to the meeting of survival needs. If we know about our world then we recognise events, and we are prepared; therefore emotional wellbeing and involvement are high.

Emotional and physical reactions start to occur in a baby as she observes the preparation of her food, the first of many transitional circumstances in her life. Focusing upon a source of food is instinctive in the initial few days of life but throughout the first 12 months a baby will develop his skill of focusing upon a chosen object (Whitebread & Basilio, 2011). A baby may commence a sucking movement and salivate prior to receiving the breast or bottle. As she matures and starts to develop a physical sense of self then the infant will raise her arms and make bouncing movements with her body. Motivation in the achievement of gross motor skills is reaching a target such as a source of food. Goals which are easy to identify and relate to physical or emotional need will encourage the young child to access opportunities to use gross and fine motor skills, and consequently gain an increase in understanding of her physical self.

Research shows that hand or arm gestures are linked to sounds and share a common neural substrate in humans (Rizzolatti & Craighero, 2004). Additionally research by Rodriguez and Palacios (2007) indicated that the mouth can be used to represent a sign to the child, as described in the practice example. Amber's open mouth symbolises the motor action which is required to complete her self-appointed task. She is supporting her problem-solving by the use of a sign rather than language. Once speech has started to develop the lip aperture used by humans may reflect the size of the subject matter during execution of motor tasks (Rizzolatti & Craighero, 2004).

Tracking actions of self and others

Mothers and fathers will instinctively talk to a baby during milk preparation, and use gestures to support self-regulation. For example, a mother will turn towards her baby as she washes her hands, prises the plastic lid from the tin of baby milk and competently accesses the row of sterilised bottles. She will lift an empty bottle to show her hungry baby, point to powdered milk, and track her own movements alongside a relevant timescale. These actions come naturally to parents who have a secure attachment and good mental health, and promote the formation of invaluable skills in regulating emotions, linking gestures, spoken word and subsequent action, and waiting with expectancy. The expectancy which is felt by a young baby who is awaiting a milk-feed by his mother or father gives him early experience of attributes linked to physical, social and teleological agency and resilience.

Whitebread and Basilio (2011) recorded the emergence of comprehensive links between gestures and routines from six months old. As the breast or bottle is lifted closer to the baby she can be observed opening and closing her mouth, and nodding, as representation of the sucking movements required for feeding. Daily routines insert order and predictability into the infant's lifestyle, and support her to understand cause and effect. These regular events in a baby's day provide multiple opportunities for the infant to begin to develop the skill of emotional regulation within a family cultural context.

The self-regulation of children from birth to six years of age was also researched (Whitebread & Basilio, 2011). Findings indicated that an ability to regulate emotions has the potential to commence in the earliest childhood years, and eventually supports the capacity to follow instructions, and to recognise and accept social boundaries, for example, in a school setting. Regular sleep/wake cycles provide an essential foundation for emotional regulation in infants and adults which support the ability to respond sensitively to the emotions of others (Byrne & Horowitz, 1981). Health visitors place great emphasis on the development of routines in the early days of childhood, and disruption to these cycles is one of the most common concerns expressed by parents to health workers and early years' practitioners.

Language acquisition

Development of the frontal lobe area of the brain begins to occur around six months of age and contributes to higher cognitive functioning of the infant (Bergen & Woodin, 2017). A baby of six months will recognise "phonemes" which these authors describe as "the smallest units of speech sounds" which occur in every language. By 12 months of age a baby will demonstrate a particular interest and focus upon "phonemes in his native language." This skill relates to familiarity of use regarding a dominant family language. Ghasemi and Hashemi (2011) studied the learning of a second language in childhood, and findings indicated that babies have the capacity to recognise and to use all sounds from the world's 6,500 languages. English has 44 sounds or phonemes. During the first year of life an infant's use of phonemes will develop by linking to meaning, and be re-termed "morphemes" which are "sounds with meaning." At 12 months an infant will use gestures which represent the function of objects alongside spoken language. He will acquire approximately 300 words by 24 months of age, and 500 words by 36 months.

Bergen and Woodin (2017) identified the eight month period in childhood as significant to development of communication and verbal language. Social referencing emerges from approximately eight months old, and the baby will interpret cultural information from the gestures of adults, particularly primary carers. The baby will acquire social rules in relation to his actions within specific contexts through observation of adults/siblings/peers.

Vocalisation is linked to a mother's communicative interaction with her infant, but the previous authors also refer to an undefined impact from different cultural expectations. Verbal interaction between mother and baby tends to follow patterns of behaviour which the mother observes in a family/community and has experienced in her own childhood years.

The current mobility in populations throughout the world may lead to merging of parenting practices between ethnicities, and I have already observed this phenomenon in early years' services. These developments enrich humankind. The circumstances can provide an invaluable social source of learning for parents by creating a focus for interaction, a focus for gaining knowledge and understanding, a focus for shared laughter as different parenting strategies are swopped, a focus for sharing the highs and lows of the most important job in the world and a focus which supports cultures to integrate.

EXAMPLE FROM PRACTICE

Aman is eight months old. She sits independently upon a black and white rug in her living-room. Aman's mother had purchased this rug at her daughter's birth as the parenting handouts from the health visitor had the same rug depicted in a photograph of a smiling mother, and her curly haired happy infant. Aman knows her family attachment figures: mother and father, sister and two brothers, two sets of doting grandparents. Aman's sister Saima is four years old, and she swings her legs in anticipation as she sits above her little sister on the low family couch. Saima giggles and waits – she knows and understands her sibling very well.

Aman can crawl but sometimes she sits on one foot, and as yet, this little girl is not quite sure of her physical self. The eight month old has made a decision. Her brown eyes open wide, and focus upon a large red ball which is nestled behind a coffee table. This ball is made of a very light plastic material, and it is adorned with farm animals and characters. These balls are useful and safe artefacts for home play but every child and parent quickly realises that the lighter the ball then the harder it is to control and to grasp with little hands.

Aman's foot is tucked in the braking position, and she lunges forward to crawl but does not make any progress. Saima jumps off the couch in one easy movement that can only be made by a competent four year old. She strokes her sister's hair, clumsily but gently, and says cheerfully, "You are stuck again!" Saima pulls her sister's foot forward; however Aman had already changed her tactics. Hindered by the trapped foot, the little learner had decided to access support – someone else would reach the ball for her. Aman rocked back and forward and stretched two hands towards her target. The infant's hands opened and closed as if practising the required motor-skills. She looked at her smiling sister, and nodded in a rhythmical way, then looked again at the ball. Direct signalling for need could not be clearer. Saima danced towards their chosen play focus and pushed the red ball into her little sister's waving arms. Saima declared with positivity and the immense pride that occurs between sisters, "You showed me what you wanted."

What does this mean in theory and practice?

Vygotsky (1978) described the emerging of a baby's perception of real-life objects from birth. The ability of a four month old infant to shape his hands appropriately preceding contact with an object was presented by Stern (1998). Recent research indicated that rhythmical hand movements accompany babbling at six–eight months old, and thereafter the ability to point emerges (Whitebread & Basilio, 2011).

Vygotsky suggested that an infant's failed attempt to grasp an object with an outstretched hand was often interpreted by a familiar adult as a deliberate gesture which represented communication by pointing. Thereafter the infant's attempts and parent's responses are linked, and the sequence is repeated, and creates a pattern of motor action. A method of communication has been established.

Alternatively, an infant who uses his hand and arm to stretch towards a desired object may be actively using the gesture to seek support from an attachment figure. These initial forward gestures by a young baby are invariably accompanied by his vocalisations, and eye contact to another being. As dexterity of finger movement develops the infant refines his use of forward gesture by tucking his thumb to palm, and using four fingers as a directional tool to indicate need. Practice and progress results in the infant using his index finger. Parents aptly apply the term "pointing finger."

The acquisition of language or an alternative communication method is a key aspect of the development of children and provides a medium which links inter- and intra-communication. Interpretation and comprehension of the world is enhanced through development of language. Rodriguez and Palacios (2007) commented that the capacity to self-regulate is supported by external regulation in the form of praise and recognition of the child's efforts from an attachment figure. The child's sense of self develops, and she gains comprehension of his impact. The next chapter focuses upon attainment and executive functioning in the early years.

References

Bergen, D., & Woodin, M. (2017). *Brain research and childhood education*. Abingdon: Routledge.

Bowlby, J. (1979). *The making and breaking of affectional bonds*. (pp. 13, 29–30, 41–45, 84–87, 124–127, 134, 154–155, 165–174, 181–187). Abingdon: Routledge.

Bratton, S. C., Landreth, G. L., Kellam, T., & Blackard, S. R. (2006). *Child/parent participation therapy treatment manual*. New York: Routledge.

Bronfenbrenner, U. (1979). *The ecology of human development* (2nd ed.). Cambridge, MA: Harvard University Press.

Byrne, J. M., & Horowitz, F. D. (1981). Rocking as soothing intervention: The influence of direction and type of movement. *Infant Behaviour and Development*. Retrieved on 6 March, 2018, from www.sciencedirect.com/science/article/pii/S0163638381800240?via%3Dihub

Ghasemi, B., & Hashemi, M. (2011). Foreign language learning during childhood. *Procedia and Behavioural Sciences, volume 28*, 872–876. Retrieved on 28 April, 2018, from www.sciencedirect.com

Iverson, J. (2010). *Developing language in a developing body: The relationship between motor development and language development*. Retrieved on 18 April, 2018, from https://doi.org/10.1017/S0305000909990432

Lave, J., & Wenger, E. (1991). *Situated learning, legitimate peripheral participation*. New York: Cambridge University Press.

Piaget, J. (2001). *The language and thought of the child. Routledge Classics, volume 52*. London: Routledge.

Rizzolatti, G., & Craighero, L. (2004). The mirror-neuron system. *Annual Review Neuroscience, volume 27*, 169–192. Retrieved on 17 December, 2017, from http://psych.colorado.edu/~kimlab/rizzolatti.annurev.neuro.2004.pdf

Rodriguez, C., & Palacios, P. (2007). Do private gestures have a self-regulatory function? A case study. *Journal of Infant Behaviour and Development, volume 30, number 2*, 180–194. Retrieved on 18 April, 2018, from https://doi.org/10.1016/j.infbeh.2007.02.010

Sanders, M. R. (1999). Triple P-positive parenting program: Towards an empirically validated multilevel parenting and family support strategy for the prevention of behaviour and emotional problems in children. *Clinical Child and Family Psychology Review, volume 2, number 2*. New York: Plenum Publishing Corporation.

Siraj-Blatchford, I., Sylva, K., Muttock, S., Gilden, R., & Bell, D. (2002). *Researching effective pedagogy in the early years, report number 356*. (pp. 8, 11, 32, 98–102, 133–135, 141). London: Department for Education and Skills.

Stern, D. N. (1998). *The interpersonal world of the infant*. London: Karnac Books Ltd.

Vivanti, G., & Rogers, S. J. (2014). Autism and the mirror neuron system: Insights from learning and teaching. *Philosophical Transactions of the Royal Society of London, Series B, Biological Science, June 5*. Retrieved on 1 April, 2018, from www.ncbi.nlm.nih.gov/pmc/articles/ PMC4006185

Vygotsky, L. (1978). *Mind in society, the development of higher psychological processes*. Cambridge, MA: Harvard University Press.

Vygotsky, L. (1986). *Thought and language*. Baskerville: The Massachusetts Institute of Technology.

Whitebread, D., & Basilio, M. (2011). The emergence and early development of self-regulation in young children. *Profesorado revista de curriculum y formacion del profeserado*. Retrieved on 7 March, 2018, from www.nhs.scot.knowledge. network

Whitters, H. G. (2018). *Family learning to inclusion: Theory, practice, and partnerships*. (pp. 54–55). Abingdon: Routledge.

Winsler et al. (2000). Verbal self-regulation over time in pre-school children at risk for attention and behaviour problems. *Journal of Child Psychology and Psychiatry, volume 41, number 7*, 875–886. Retrieved on 25 December, 2017, from www.researchgate.net/publication/12249166_Verbal_Self.

Yirka, B. (2015). *Suffixation influences receivers' behaviour in non-human primates*. Retrieved on 1 April, 2018, from www.phys.org/news/2015-04-monkey-species-html

4 Attainment and executive functioning

This chapter discusses the principles of working memory, response inhibition, self-regulation and task-shifting. These issues are explored in a context of research and practice which focus upon the link between executive functioning, and relationships with an attachment figure of parent or professional.

Executive functioning – what is it?

Executive functioning can be interpreted in practice as purposeful involvement with a learning environment which involves the use of deep level learning. There are many research studies on this human skill, and findings agree upon the three main components: working memory, response inhibition and attention/task-shifting (Pauen et al., 2016).

There are few research studies on executive functioning in early childhood due to difficulty in designing test tasks for the purpose of data collection. Pre-planned learning environments are not the most effective medium in which to support a child's demonstration of executive functioning and actualisation of potential.

The findings of Pauen et al. (2016) are significant to strategic and operational planning, and create a link between skills associated with executive functioning in childhood and outcomes within adulthood. This research indicated that self-control in childhood is more important than socio-economic status or IQ in predicting adult' physical health, wealth and parenting skills. Diamond and Lee (2011) granted greater significance to the executive functions of problem-solving, reasoning and planning for identifying school-readiness than IQ. Research on the economics of inequality highlights the powerful impact of cognition *and* social skills upon equality and achievement (Heckman, 2011).

Other studies have associated executive functioning to a range of outcomes in childhood and adulthood (Center on Developing Child, 2012).

- Achievement in school and workplace – fulfilment of personal or an organisation's goals requires ability and capacity to follow instructions, to plan and execute and to adapt behaviour to meet social expectations within different contexts.
- Good physical and mental health, and associated behaviours – good health requires the individual to know himself and his needs, to make positive choices which support his ability and capacity to function effectively, and to operate purposefully as an individual, and within a social context.

Diamond (2002) identified that executive functions will change over time, qualitatively and quantitatively due to maturing of the brain and the effect of environmental influences. This chapter explores the link between a secure attachment relationship, learning opportunities and executive functioning within services and the home environment.

Working memory, response inhibition and task-shifting

This section will explore the theory and practice of the core concepts which are associated with executive functioning: "working memory," "response inhibition" and "task-shifting." These concepts are separate but inter-connected (Garon et al., 2008; Pauen & Early Development of Self-Regulation Group, 2016), and the discussion will incorporate the impact from, and upon "self-regulation." Authors may vary these terms, for example the research team at Harvard refer to "working memory," "self-control" and "mental flexibility" (Center on Developing Child, 2012).

Working memory

Working memory is the result of processes which a human being uses to decide upon relevance of new knowledge. The inner working model guides actions and behaviour through reference to information which is gained from interpretation of the environment. Sorting and processing of information is influenced by emotions, and motivation for learning which may lead to re-configuration of the previous base of knowledge and understanding.

Activation of working memory involves a child or adult demonstrating an increased level of functioning due to awareness of change and the capacity to extrapolate, to discard, to retain or to scaffold knowledge. This process results in a change to comprehension, and supports prioritisation of information for immediate or potential use.

Explicit and implicit memories

Memories are known to be created by external stimulus in the form of environmental features which can act as prompts to invoke prior circumstances and associated actions – "explicit memories." Memories are also created by internal stimulus in the form of emotions which accompany, and influence interactions – "implicit memories." These emotions are linked to learning through sensory experiences. Everyone is familiar with memory triggers which are based upon auditory stimulus, for example, favourite music, tactile stimulus from materials/clothing or perhaps olfactory and salivary stimulus in anticipation of familiar food and drink.

Working memory is widely regarded as the first component of executive functioning, and research and practice indicate that infants aged birth to six months can retain simple representations of their world. These latent memories tend to be formed in a context of repetitive daily routines which encompass the earliest days of life, for example feeding, changing and nurturing. The young infant will display memory through behaviour which demonstrates his ability to accurately predict routines, and actions of others within specific contexts. From six months to two years of age the child will gradually refine his skills in updating and manipulating information, dealing with simple conflict and coordinating working memory and his response inhibitions. Patterns of interaction between the child and his carers emerge over time.

EXAMPLE FROM PRACTICE

Routines for learning

Nalen is a young father in charge of the bed-time routine. His son, Dinuka, is 18 months old. A sturdy toddler with tight black curls, a massive smile, and unquenchable thirst for knowledge of his world. Dinuka's day is composed of short regular routines which respond to the needs of this developing toddler – eat, play, rest and lots of nurturing from his primary carers and large extended family. Dinuka sits on a purple bean-bag chair, the soft material moulds to his shape, comfortably familiar and accommodating his preferred position. The little boy rests contentedly as he observes his mother clearing remnants of the evening meal, the final dishes clatter on the metal sink, and he recognises the wiping of surfaces as the prelude to the next stage of this nightly adventure.

The sound of water splashing! His father coughing as steam fills the small bathroom. Hot and cold water clash, and herald the filling of a child's bath. Dinuka's sleepy state has changed within seconds, and he wriggles away from the enveloping bean-bag chair. "Dinuka, bring your towel please." This learner remembers the routine, he knows the sequence of events, expectations are easy to understand, easy to accomplish in his family context. Each stage is a goal achieved. Repetitive actions are exciting, and fill young children and their parents with pride. "Working memory" – Dinuka runs to the low towel rack – it's empty! Then he spots the washing basket at the back-door and retrieves a fluffy towel – "shifting within a task." Dinuka walks quickly towards his father, tripping a little as the bath towel unfolds. Nalen grins broadly as father and son continue on their learning journey.

What does this mean in theory and practice?

Bathing children is a necessary aspect of parenting, but the learning opportunities which evolve from regular scenarios are multiple, and if capitalised upon then they can contribute greatly to a child's use of working memory, compilation of skills and executive functioning. An additional outcome is affirmation of a secure attachment relationship.

Levels of working memory can be differentiated and demonstrated through simple, and complex tasks as described in the research study by Garon et al. (2008):

- "Simple working memory tasks" incur the child retaining information as memories over a period of time.
- "Complex working memory tasks" incur the child retaining information, and using it to change his or her knowledge base. For example, Dinuka had learned that his bath towel could be found every night upon the towel-rack but he adapted admirably to an unexpected change of circumstances – his inner working model was altered by this occurrence.

Re-configuration of the inner working model takes place in children and adults in response to interpretation and assimilation of knowledge. This process requires the use of complex working memory, and results in a change or adaptation to actions and behaviour.

Working memory contributes to each person's ability to override behavioural and emotional responses, and leads to successful self-regulation of behaviour. Kuczynski and Kochanska (1990) identified that simple response inhibition, the ability to suppress a dominant response, develops in the first 12 months after birth, and continues to evolve over time. The research findings indicated that this skill is acquired rapidly by an infant within the first three years of life.

- 8 month olds can inhibit behaviour 40% of time
- 22 month olds can inhibit behaviour 78% of time
- 33 month olds can inhibit behaviour 90% of time

Research by Hofmann et al. (2012) also showed interesting results which reflect current practise, and the pedagogical approach of incorporating active learning alongside scaffolding of knowledge by peers and adults. The use of "simple working memory" links to automatic affective reactions which are based upon emotions, and result in the activation of motor schemas. Practitioners describe these actions as behaviour which demonstrates a child's emotions – behavioural communication. Parents eliminate the emotional influence from their interpretation, and describe the actions as "impulsive and performed without any thought or meaning."

It is always a useful source of learning for professionals to listen to expressions which are applied by parents in describing their children's actions. The wording clearly displays the knowledge base of parents with regard to their children's interpretations, communication and needs. Alternatively findings indicated that the capacity to use "complex working memory"

maintains attention to tasks and supports a person to resist diversion to stimuli at an early stage of information processing.

Executive functioning becomes sophisticated over time, and evolves from the coordination of the simple cognitive skills which are observable in the early years, for example, object recognition and developing a sense of the physical self by reaching and pointing towards goals. Accumulation and refinement of skills leads to a change in the child's internal state which influences interactions based upon a deep level of learning.

Response inhibition

Self-regulation

Pauen et al. (2016) describe self-regulation as a purposeful mental activity which impacts upon and changes cognitive, emotional or motivational processes. Emotions and motivational ability tend to be connected. The rationale for self-regulation is the necessity for adaptation in accordance with physical, emotional or social needs which are pertinent to a specific situation.

Young children are initially dependent upon adult care-givers to support regulation of internal states but gradually inter-personal regulation is replaced by intra-personal regulation. Fischer and Hencke (1996) found potential conflict between old and new skills but over time coordination and higher performance output is achieved. Infants of 6–12 months show an ability to react effectively to low levels of conflict, and behaviour is progressively directed by internal choice-making as opposed to external factors. The infant develops the early stages of self-regulation in goal-directed behaviours; however, throughout childhood and adulthood, human beings may continue to demonstrate dependency upon others to support this area of functioning.

Garon et al. (2008) also compared simple and complex response inhibition, and clarified aspects of the two skill-sets.

- Simple response inhibition involves the child "withholding or delaying" a response.
- Complex response inhibition involves the child "inhibiting" an automatic response, and subsequently using new information to "change" his response.

Research terms can be challenging to link to practice which often applies different terms for a similar occurrence. For the purpose of this chapter self-control relates to simple response inhibition, and self-regulation to complex response inhibition.

By three-to-five years of age the child's skill of self-regulation has matured considerably, and she will demonstrate an ability to recognise, and to respond to complex rules as applied within different environments (Zelazo, 2005). Research studies indicate that the child's length and frequency of attention to task increases steadily from birth to five years (Lansink & Mintz, 2000), and the process is accompanied by an ability to resolve conflict (Posner & Rothbart, 2001).

EXAMPLE FROM PRACTICE

Response inhibition

Olga is two years of age. She has recently commenced nursery, and quickly decided that the chute is her favourite activity. Attending nursery is Olga's first formal social experience, and she is faced with multiple challenges. Chutes are common examples of physical equipment which supports many skill-sets in the earliest years. This particular chute can be configured in different ways as the manufacturer has created multiple coloured pieces which slot firmly together to form challenges for young explorers. Gross motor skills, eye-foot coordination, spatial awareness, social rules, cooperative play, imaginative play, and the concept of fast v slow are some of the many developmental milestones which can result from the "chute experience" in early years' services. The practitioners in this nursery had carefully coordinated the colours of each piece of the chute to provide prompts and guidance for social turn-taking, and safe use of equipment. Climb up the green steps and down the red slide!

Olga's working memory is activated but immature – this is her first encounter with rules of engagement. Olga's motivation is the experience of the red slide so it makes sense to this little planner to immediately turn around at the bottom of the slide and attempt to climb back up – much quicker than finding the green steps and waiting in line to negotiate the obstacle to her goal!

The two year old resisted physical prompting by her key-worker, and protested loudly. Eventually a practitioner competently and swiftly lifted the little girl towards the green steps, and supported rapid goal achievement by guiding Olga up and down again. Olga laughed and turned towards the red slide again but she paused on this occasion, as a mountaineer contemplating an ascent, and glanced at a practitioner. The use of another verbal reminder and prompting by pointing supported the early stages of working memory, response inhibition and set-shifting.

What does this mean in theory and practice?

During "response inhibition" a child activates two different processes within the context of self-regulating his or her behaviour.

1 "Self-control" – Olga controls expression of her inner state. This means that the child actively stops herself demonstrating a particular behaviour. The behaviour would have represented her initial interpretation of a situation, her emotional reaction and her motor response.
2 "Self-regulation" – The child shifts her focus, and demonstrates a different behaviour. This means that she is actively inhibiting dominant or automatic responses, and "shifting" to another mental set, and associated behaviour. Shifting requires the use of working memory. A child has to have awareness of her behaviour in order to suppress actions, and to switch focus. In early childhood this awareness is given to the child from adults.

The five developmental stages to achievement of the autobiographical self in the earliest years were explored in chapter one: physical agent, social agent, teleological agent, intentional mental agent, and autobiographical self (Trevarthan & Aitken, 2001). Infants and children can easily be supported through these steps in practice within services and the home environment.

Implementation of the curriculum within settings inherently incorporates opportunities for children to develop and to refine skills associated with self-regulation; however, practitioners may not be aware of the significance of song-time, the use of musical instruments, ring-games, snack, book and small world corner, imaginative, creative and cooperative play indoors and outdoors. For example, supporting young children to start, to stop, and to start again as they run up a grassy hill, encouraging children to wait, to observe, and to receive their snack within a group of peers, asking children to hit a drum hard then soft and hard once more, promoting the use of a loud voice and a quiet whisper during small world play and participating in a game of hide and seek are common daily examples of activities used by every early years' practitioner. Planned and unplanned exercises are valid learning opportunities which nurture the development of self-regulation in early childhood through promotion of the physical, social and intellectual self.

Practitioners and parents may interpret a child's behaviour as "testing social boundaries," but complex processes are difficult to master in childhood, and achievement of skill requires repetition and refinement over time. Attention to task is a basic building block for operation of the executive functioning system (Barkley, 1998). An environment which clearly presents and promotes social rules, care-givers who prompt and guide a child responsively and consistently, and share the child's motivation to achieve a goal are factors which enhance opportunities for executive functioning. This represents Olga's nursery experience.

Goldberg et al. (2002) identified that development of the frontal cortex is dependent on influences from the environment, which may be negative or positive, which he termed "environmental remediation." Many studies express that executive functioning is a "trainable" skill; however, in the early years' context the concept of training children is not applicable. Whether the child is in the infant, toddler or pre-school stage, skill development is supported through environmental stimulation, broad learning opportunities and nurturing the child's sense of autobiographical self within a secure attachment relationship. For example, Olga was constructively supported to increase her attention to the processes involved in her goal achievement by environmental prompts and guidance from her key worker. Recognition and celebration of her final objective was shared by the little girl and supportive carer in nursery.

As Olga attempted to climb up the slide for the second time it was significant that the practitioner reduced her intervention strategy. The practitioner replaced physical prompting with pointing and verbal confirmation of the social rule. Practice must encourage and allow children to develop their executive skills within each activity, and to become independent operators. Skills can develop in a short timescale and the child's achievement should be verbally tracked and positively reinforced.

Professional reflection

Professional reflection and peer feedback is promoted within the work of early years' teams, and an integral aspect is taking time to explore and to discuss the decision-making of children. Planned and spontaneous opportunities should be used for seniors, key workers and student to learn from one another. Typically a student will be able to accurately describe a child's participation in an activity in great detail – students tend to conduct observations, and will have time to focus upon individual children due to course requirements. Observations equip a team with knowledge of each child's operational skills and the means to interpret the infant's perspective of her world in order to support development within a service, and home environment. The key worker will put the activity into context, and use the information to assess and to re-evaluate the child's developmental level.

It is invaluable for early years' workers to observe the intricate processes of executive functioning in order to inform individual learning plans. This comprehension of the child's operational ability can influence adaptation of the environmental stimulus and/or change the interactive approach by a supportive carer. The senior will seek out deep understanding from research and theory to share with the team and to complement the practitioner's perspective. I have often been part of enlightening discussions with teams which take place at the end of a long working day. Staff are tired and ready to go home but willing and keen to share examples of children's prowess. A few moments of interaction can result in immense value for professional development.

Self-regulation impairment

Social and emotional factors

It is important to understand negative influences upon ability and capacity to self-regulate. Circumstances can create adversities, for example, cognitive overload, low self-esteem, environmental and social factors. Failure to self-regulate can also relate to a lack of goals for oneself or a lack of motivation or capacity. Research has identified a significant feature of adverse childhood experiences (ACEs) as inconsistent and non-responsive care-giving or negative care-giving (Scottish Government, 2018). These circumstances can result in insecure attachment between primary carer and child.

The activation of self-control can have a positive or negative impact upon a human being. Gaining understanding and demonstrating appropriate contextual behaviour is positive due to social acceptance and an increase in learning opportunities; however, the processes used to achieve these outcomes can be arduous and reduce personal resources. A period of positive social behaviour may well be followed by a child's negative expressive actions due to the immense energy which is used for these functions; therefore there may be a negative effect upon subsequent acts of self-control. Prolonged periods of high level interactions of learning can also result in episodes of negative behaviours.

Changing one's actions and operating with intent and purpose takes time and opportunities to practise. Learning experiences in relation to self-regulation achieve maximum effect if they are set within a framework for development of the autobiographical self.

- Practising physical regulation within daily activities is the necessary prelude to social and emotional regulation.
- Understanding cause and effect emerges from experiential play and an increase in awareness of one's own impact upon the physical world.
- Teleological agency supports comprehension of self as an intentional mental agent and encompasses knowledge of society's social codes and expectations of behaviour.
- Operating as the autobiographical self, albeit within immaturity of childhood, is a complex achievement which can only be realised if each step is supported by an attachment figure.

The *failure* of self-regulation is often described in publications; however 100% achievement on every occasion is not always feasible due to unpredictable external and internal influences upon a child. Children and adults can be supported through these processes by an attentive and responsive carer or practitioner. A powerful motivator in childhood and adulthood is demonstration of another person's belief in your ability and capacity to learn, particularly within the context of a meaningful relationship. A common strategy in current services is recognition of emotions alongside actions, and positive affirmation of the child's sense of self. Verbalising a child's involvement with learning and wellbeing status can act as prompts to support transferability of skills. Parenting programmes, for example, The Positive Parenting Programme (Triple P) clearly promote this understanding to parents (Sanders, 1999) and advocate responsive parenting strategies.

Research has shown links between a temporary reduction in blood glucose and low executive functioning. Consuming glucose can boost performance on working memory capacity and inhibition tasks within a short time-frame (Hofmann et al., 2012). Humans have a natural inclination to respond to changes in blood sugar levels by seeking out sustenance and hydration; however, immaturity of a child, lack of communication ability and emotional status can create barriers to children accessing support in response to physiological need. Recent educational practice in the United Kingdom and elsewhere promotes the regular availability of water and snacks for each child during the nursery or school day. Workplaces also provide water outlets to employees, and there is a clear understanding of the link between hydration and brain function.

Task/Set-shifting

The ability to focus upon a task encompasses the capacity to minimise potential distraction from external or internal influences. This phenomenon was described by Iguchi et al. (2005) as both enhancing goal-specific information and reducing irrelevant information. Infants from birth can demonstrate an ability to select a stimulus and to focus attention, which is usually related to basic nurturing needs. Between one and two years an infant's behaviour starts to be influenced by internal voluntary factors which respond to the demand of the task. As the child matures the use of her working memory, and inhibition mechanisms, will gradually support her to pursue a goal by minimising external or internal distraction.

Practice in the early years should always consider internal and external influences – a child's health, wellbeing and emotional status/response, in addition to environmental stimulus. Family learning frameworks promote partnership-working between primary and secondary carers (Education Scotland, 2018). Drop-off and pick-up time in nursery or school are ideal points of contact for information sharing, short discussions, promoting understanding and seeking out strategies from one another. This forum leads to the creation of a rich base for each child's educational journey which is built upon knowledge and understanding of internal and external influences with particular relevance to a specific day or time-period.

EXAMPLE FROM PRACTICE

Many parents and early years' services purchase pop-up toys for children in the first eighteen months of life. Commonly the pop-up toy is composed of strong, multi-coloured plastic – traditionally four animals in a row, and hidden under four lids with pop-up mechanisms. Easy to transport and ideal for stationary play, for example, a non-ambulant infant, on car journeys, high-chairs or push-chairs.

Upon analysis this toy requires the infant to have a complex set of skills – "working memory," "self-regulation" and "task-shifting" in order to activate each level of play which leads to "executive functioning." There are four options of increasing difficulty which manufacturers always position from right to left – assuming that children will use their right hand although this presentation is not actually relevant to children in the first few years.

- Option 1 = *a round button is easily activated by pressure on any point, and immediately the child will receive the return of an animal popping out of a box*
- Option 2 = *a roller switch requires pressure on one side only, in order to achieve the goal*
- Option 3 = *a knob for turning requires the ability to use thumb and forefinger but usefully this option will activate with a small quarter turn*
- Option 4 = *the most complex level of dexterity is required to turn a knob 360 degrees and release before the animal pops up to welcome the child.*

A myriad of skills, and processes are used by the young child in this seemingly simple and commonly used toy: sensory feedback as auditory and tactile stimulus, remembering and applying information appropriately to activate each mechanism, recognition of position and use of fist, palm or thumb and index finger, and emotional investment. Most children have a favourite animal but will activate each option from right to left until their chosen goal is reached. After much practising the keen explorer will identify a shortcut, and show ability to access his favourite animal without using any prior steps.

What does this mean in theory and practice?

Research has identified set-shifting as the most complex component of executive functioning. Complexity relates to the reliance on set-shifting for building upon a foundation of working memory and response inhibition. Garon et al. (2008) apply the term "set-shifting" to describe two processes in response inhibition.

- The child creates and remembers (working memory) a link between a particular stimulus and her response,
- then she gains additional knowledge,
- she inhibits behaviour (response inhibition),
- and finally, she shifts to a new internal mental set (set-shifting).

Hofmann et al. (2012) extended this comprehension of set-shifting by promoting the need for children to move back and forward between tasks or mental states in order to refine their skills. The zone of proximal development was described by Vygotsky (1978) as being in advance of what is already known. Repetition and practice is the route to achieving this status for human beings, and the journey can incur the use of lower and higher levels of functioning together. Bowlby (1979) referred to the outcome of these processes as re-configuration of the inner working model. This means that the reference base of knowledge and understanding which guides the actions of a human being has changed; therefore his actions also change. Learning and development in children and adults involves multiple set-shifting; for example, the pop-up toy has four set-shifts.

Key workers in a nursery may express that there is limited time in a busy early years' schedule to "properly observe" and to assess children's needs and abilities. A snapshot observation can be conducted in minutes within any circumstances. Focussing upon the minutiae provides rich detail to support developmental assessments. For example, an infant's interpretation and interaction with a pop-up toy can deliver information on fine motor skills, attention or diversion focus, working memory, capacity to adapt, social behaviours, self-control, set-shifting, self-regulation, goal-setting and recognition of achievement, in addition to responsivity to attachment cues from a primary carer.

The research by Zelazo (2005) indicated that children may have difficulty in stopping behaviour in one mental set in order to re-configure and change to another set. Knowledge and understanding may be acquired, but development involves coordination of a new skill with the old. Optimum practice provides opportunities for slow, predictable changes between sets. Implementation of the curriculum by supporting children to scaffold knowledge, and to identify and use personal learning styles, is the response in practice to these findings.

Task-shifting can be beneficial or maladaptive to self-regulation. Outcomes are dependent upon the environmental context, motivation of the child, and socio-cultural factors (Hofmann et al., 2012). Research conducted in 2016 extended the practice information which can be gleaned from previous findings. The study included secure attachment and social interaction with a care-giver as contributory to self-regulation (Pauen & Early Development of Self-Regulation Group, 2016). Research is ever-evolving and the research community throughout the world is inter-dependent. Each study is set in a particular context, and findings provide knowledge and activate curiosity in fellow researchers which provokes further study of a topic.

Rest and down-regulation

In 2013 Bernier et al. (2013) conducted research on potential links between sleep and cognition. The study indicated an association with length of sleep periods and levels of cognitive performance in adults. The explanation for these findings described cellular and biochemical mechanisms which take place in the brain during sleep, and support brain plasticity and ultimately the consolidation of learning. The research also encompassed a sample set of children under five years, and indicated that night-time sleep periods during the earliest years relate to executive functioning in later years of childhood. The study promotes sleep and rest as essential aspects of healthy brain development in children and their parents. Sleep routines of young infants and their parents tend to coincide during the early years due to a need for care and supervision.

Sleepless nights is the common cry of parents, and a tired mother or father finds it challenging to provide optimum care and stimulation for a little child. Practitioners can encourage parents and carers to take additional rest during the time that children attend nurseries or school. We all welcome permission to focus upon our needs and encouragement to maintain our own health and wellbeing. Daily chats between parent and professionals can promote educational messages within informal interactions.

Most children develop self-calming strategies in the earliest days of childhood. Parents are usually aware of these techniques, for example, a young baby may gain comfort and emotional stability from sensory feedback such as rubbing the silk labels on her clothing. This stimulus may continue to be sought throughout childhood and perhaps in adulthood, albeit in a different form. Pauen et al. (2016) referred to the outcome as "down-regulation," which links to the induced soporific effect.

Seeking out knowledge of the world is challenging and exciting for children but also tiring, and effective learning environments encourage quiet times which support the brain to assimilate and to sort information. Early years' services and primary schools provide rest stations for children, often promoted as "chill-out areas," perhaps within pop-up tents. A few minutes of rest away from stimulation can be hugely beneficial to children's capacity to retain learning. During periods of rest and sleep the brain is actively working to create and sustain neural connections.

Some children are reluctant to rest within a play environment, and it is essential that practitioner use their ingenuity to create opportunities which reduce stimulation, even for a short period. Examples are large story books which entail children lying or sitting down to participate, listening to classical music, the use of sensory equipment or similar artefacts in a playroom, songs which involve periods of rest or induce stillness for a few moments, or even hide and seek with extended times for hiding in order to encourage intrepid adventurers to rest within the game. Asking children to shut their eyes during these activities can support a young body to gain solace from the vibrant, stimulating atmosphere of an early years' service and to achieve "down-regulatory capacity." Reactive practice recognises and responds to the internal and external needs of each child, and these features make a practitioner's role challenging, and fulfilling.

Attachment relationship and up-regulation

Many years ago Vygotsky (1978) emphasised the importance of external support to induce internalisation and regulation of inner states of the child. The research studies by Fay-Stammbach et al. (2014) recently promoted the importance of this input from care-givers in relation to the child's development of a sense of self. "Up-regulation" as termed by Pauen et al. (2016) can be activated through distraction, instruction or a change of perspective. The early years' workforce are adept at spontaneous and planned distraction or task-shifting to support children's focus of attention, and research provides the rationale for these daily strategies which can be observed in every establishment. This knowledge and understanding of daily practice strategies which is gained from research leads to consistency, repeatability and applicability over time, and environments.

References

Barkley, R. A. (1998). *Attention-deficit hyperactivity disorder: A handbook for diagnosis*. Retrieved on 17 June, 2018, from www.ncbi.nlm.nih.gov/pmc/articles/PMC2247447/

Bernier, A., Beauchamp, M. H., Bouvette-Turcot, A.-A., Carrier, J., & Carlson, S. M. (2013). Sleep and cognition in pre-school years, specific links to executive functioning. *Child Development, volume 84, number 5, September/October*. Retrieved on 3 December, 2017, from http://onlinelibrary.wiley.com.knowledge.idm.oclc.org/doi/10.1111/cdev.12063/full

Bowlby, J. (1979). *The making and breaking of affectional bonds*. (pp. 13, 29–30, 41–45, 84–87, 124–127, 134, 154–155, 165–174, 181–187). Abingdon: Routledge.

Center on Developing Child at Harvard University. (2012). *Executive functioning* (In brief). Retrieved on 30 November, 2017, from https://developingchild.harvard.edu/science/key-concepts/executive-function/

Diamond, A. (2002). *Normal development of prefrontal cortex from birth to young adulthood: Cognitive functions, anatomy, and biochemistry*. New York: Oxford University Press.

Diamond, A., & Lee, K. (2011). Interventions shown to aid executive function development in children 4–12 years old. *Science, August 19*, 959–964. Retrieved on 28 May, 2018, from www.nhs.scot.knowledge.network

Education Scotland. (2018). *Family learning framework, advice for practitioners*. Retrieved on 8 June, 2018, from http://nationalarchives.gov.uk/open-government-licence

Fay-Stammbach, T. (2014). *Parenting influences on executive function in early childhood*. Retrieved on 17 June, 2018, from https://onlinelibrary.wiley.com/doi/abs/10.1111/cdep.12095

Fischer, K. W., & Hencke, R. W. (1996). Infant's construction of actions in context: Paiget's contribution to research on early development. *Psychological Bulletin, volume 7, number 4, July*. Retrieved on 28 May, 2018, from www.nhs.scot.knowledge.network

Garon, N., Bryson, S. E., & Smith, I. M. (2008). Executive function in pre-schoolers: A review using an integrative framework. *Psychological Bulletin, volume 134, number 1*. Retrieved on 7 December, 2017, from www.nhs.scot.knowledge.network

Goldberg, M. E., Bisley, J., Powell, K. D., Gottlieb, J., & Kusunoki, M. (2002). The role of the lateral intraparietal area of the monkey in the generation of saccades and visuospatial attention. *Annual New York Academical Science, volume 956*, 205–215. Retrieved on 17 June, 2018, from www.nhs.scot.knowledge.network

Heckman, J. J. (2011). The economics of inequality, the value of early childhood education. *American Educator, Spring*, 1–47. Retrieved on 1 May, 2017, from www.nhs.scot.knowledge.network

Hofmann, W., Schmeichel, B. J., & Baddeley, A. D. (2012). Executive functions and self-regulation. *Trends in Cognitive Sciences*. Retrieved on 25 December, 2017, from www.researchgate.net/publication/221834532_Executive_functions_and_self-regulation

Iguchi, Y., Hoshi, Y., Tanosaki, M., Taira, M., & Hashimoto, I. (2005). Attention induces reciprocal activity in the human somatosensory cortex enhancing relevant and suppressing irrelevant inputs from fingers. *Clinical Neurophysiology, volume 116*, 1077–1087. Retrieved on 12 December, 2017, from www.nhs.scot.knowledge.network

Kuczynski, L., & Kochanska, G. (1990). Development of children's noncompliance strategies from toddlerhood to age 5. *Developmental Psychology, volume 26, number 3*, 398–408. Retrieved on 28 May, 2018, from http://dx.doi.org/10.1037/0012-1649.26.3.398

Lansink, J. M., & Mintz, S. (2000). The distribution of infant attention during object examination. *Developmental Science, volume 3, number 2*, 163–170. Retrieved on 17 June, 2018, from http://jerlab.psych.sc.edu/pdf/expt30

Pauen, S., & Early Development of Self-Regulation Group (EDOS). (2016). Understanding early development of self-regulation and co-regulation: EDOS and Process of Self and Co-Regulation (PROSECO). *Journal of Self-Regulation and Regulation, volume 2*. Retrieved on 31 December, 2017, from www.nhs.scot.knowledge.network

Posner, M. I., & Rothbart, M. K. (2001). Research on attention networks as a model for the integration of psychological science. *Annual Review Psychology, number 58, December 19, 2017*, 1–23. Retrieved on 17 June, 2018, from www.researchgate.net/publication/6764747_Posner_MI_Rothbart_MK

Sanders, M. R. (1999). Triple P-positive parenting program: Towards an empirically validated multilevel parenting and family support strategy for the prevention of behaviour and emotional problems in children. *Clinical Child and Family Psychology Review, volume 2, number 2*. New York: Plenum Publishing Corporation.

Scottish Government. (2018). *What have ACEs got to do with justice?* Retrieved on 8 June, 2018, from www.gov.scot

Trevarthan, C., & Aitken, K. J. (2001). Infant intersubjectivity: Research, theory, and clinical applications. *Journal of Child Psychology and Psychiatry, volume 42.* Cambridge: Cambridge University Press.

Vygotsky, L. S. (1978). *Mind in society, the development of higher psychological processes.* (pp. 56, 86). Cambridge, MA: Harvard University Press.

Zelazo, P. D. (2005). *Development of affective decision making for self and others.* Retrieved on 17 June, 2018, from http://journals.sagepub.com/doi/10.1111/j.0956-7976.2005.01564

5 Inter-generational impact and executive functioning

This chapter discusses an inter-generational impact upon executive functioning by reference to recent research and highlights the significance of family learning and early intervention. Three levels of stress response are presented in a context of brain development, and the chapter concludes with key messages.

Inter-generational impact

Adverse childhood experiences

The Adverse Childhood Experience Studies indicate links between exposure to dysfunctionality in the household during the earliest years and risk factors for death in adulthood (Felitti et al., 1998). Additionally, Heatherton and Wagner (2011) identified self-regulatory failure in adults as central to many mental and associated physical health conditions. The foundation of self-control and regulation of behaviour in accordance with social expectations is created in the earliest years. Impulsive behaviour in childhood is a recorded risk factor for criminality (Scottish Government, 2018).

A current publication by the Scottish Government (2018) clearly connects adverse childhood experiences and the justice system in relation to victims, witnesses and perpetrators. The report indicates that minimising the effect from adversities in childhood could significantly impact crime reduction. The five most commonly cited sources of adversity upon children are encompassed within child protection policy and legislation – physical, verbal and sexual abuse and physical/emotional neglect. The Scottish report also publicises the five most common household adversities as mental illness, incarcerated relative, domestic violence, parental separation and substance abuse.

Family learning

Research conducted at Harvard University identifies three sources of influences which can affect brain architecture, and ultimately learning and development: genetics, environment and experiences (National Scientific Council on the Developing Child, 2014). Belsky and Pluess (2009) emphasised that brain plasticity is an outcome of the influences from both nature and nurture. It has been established that the first thousand days of life present an opportune period for learning, but the human brain does continue to process information for executive functioning throughout the lifespan. Although the period of pre-birth to three years is known to be a sensitive time for neural connections to occur, the property of plasticity provides potential for increasing brain function. These findings have direct implications for policy and practice in the field, and indicate the need for timely personalised responding to a service-user's reaction to adversities (Belsky & Pluess, 2013).

Attainment

Early intervention should be family focused, and aim to support change and development in parents, children and extended family. Practising in a context of three generations of a family, for example grandparents, birth parents and child, gives opportunities for positive inter-generational impact.

Genetically the human brain is programmed to develop in the optimum order to achieve potential. Lower levels of functioning are established first, for example, actions which are based upon social and emotional development. The higher levels of functioning are built upon this foundation, and encompass cognition, problem-solving and self-regulation. The ability to assess and evaluate each child's operational functions is a key professional skill for early years' workers. In the practice context it is essential that experienced senior staff observe and assess children alongside appointed key workers. Seniors may regularly review records which key workers have completed, but responsive and successful intervention is dependent on supervision of practice in situ, and identification of the appropriate approach within services, and at home.

The context of assessment, auditing and accountability within a service can result in the practitioner maintaining a narrow focus upon executive functioning, and attainment in relation to each child which is specific to a time-frame. Daily, weekly or monthly key worker observations present achievement and steps to development for every child, but gaining a comprehensive understanding of the rationale and wider long-term implications of executive functioning is essential.

The primary outcome of executive functioning is attainment in daily living in addition to achieving educational goals, but it is important to consider the link between crime reduction and the particular skills associated with executive functioning: working memory, self-regulation and task/set-shifting. Practitioners in the early years can gain insight into the significance of their daily interactions with children by referring to research which presents the impact upon the individual, and society, and also future generations of a family.

For example, findings by Bodrova et al. (2011) indicated that symbolic play supported self-regulation. Throughout every nation, in each nursery or school, carers and educators set up home corners for imaginative play. Developmental milestones are observed and recorded, and strengths or weaknesses are discussed as play evolves in this pseudo-home setting; however, further interpretation of outcomes, and implications, should be sought by the professional. The minutiae of play encompasses learning which has a life-time impact upon self and others. A deeper level of comprehension will support the workforce to link common practice to theory of executive functioning, and ultimately attainment.

I believe that this area of work is a key example of a potential implementation gap which can be minimised by each organisation. Research indicates that policy should respond to the issues at three levels – individual, family and community (Scottish Government, 2018). Practice can easily follow this strategic approach at the operational level through the implementation of early intervention in an inter-generational context which is currently known as family learning (Whitters, 2018).

Stress

Inter-generational intervention should take into account the reaction of each family member to adversities in a context of stress and the implications for operational value of a family unit. Theory, and practice frameworks can be used to understand the formation of perceptions, and consequently actions, behaviour and emotions. The association of stress and childhood years is based upon research from the field of neuroscience. "Stress" is a term which is applied to many formal and informal contexts in our society, and it is useful for practitioners to gain comprehension of this concept, and the implementation of a curriculum within an early intervention service.

There are three levels of stress which are associated with human beings in the earliest years and throughout adulthood, and refer to an impact upon the body from the stress response system, and not to an actual event (Center on the Developing Child, 2017; National Scientific Council on the Developing Child, 2014):

1. Positive stress
2. Tolerable stress
3. Toxic stress

Positive stress

The effect of "positive stress" is short-term, and learning how to cope with the body's reaction to daily adversities, at this low level, is an important aspect of maintaining good mental health. Coping mechanisms which are acquired by children are often termed "resilience" in a context of early years' work. A slight raising of the body's stress hormone, in the form of cortisol, will take place but regulation is achievable by the individual. Repeated exposure to low level stresses within daily living minimises the negative reaction upon the human body over time.

Tolerable stress

Brain architecture can be affected by "tolerable stress" but secure attachment relationships support the child to self-regulate his or her reaction and return to physical and mental stability within a short time-period. The brain can recover from this negative influence. This level of stress can often occur as a result of a life-crisis event, for example a bereavement, illness or change of circumstances.

Toxic stress

"Toxic stress" is prolonged activation of the body's stress responses which can have a long-term impact upon the brain architecture, development and executive functioning. Memory is often impaired as a result of exposure to toxic stress, and abnormal patterns of cortisol production can also occur. This level of stress may result from an internal influence in the form of emotional reaction to adversity and/or external influence in the form of mental and physical abuse or neglect (Whitters, 2017).

Stress responses

The inter-generational impact is strikingly apparent in family services as children may reflect and adopt the stress reactions which they observe in parents or grandparents (Whitters, 2018).

Early years' professionals often work with siblings or children who are related through an extended family network. Practice knowledge also highlights variable responses to stress by these children despite the common context, and this grants significance to personalised responding to each child by an attachment figure. Secure attachment is promoted throughout services as a key factor in a child's development of resilience to adversity, and subsequently increasing executive functioning skills throughout the lifespan.

Stress regulation is promoted naturally by a responsive primary carer to a young infant from birth; however, a mother or father who has experienced negativities prior to parenthood may not have the capacity or ability to demonstrate reciprocal care. If a mother or father's interpretation of the world results in toxic stress then these primary carers will not be able to support their child to self-regulate.

The stress response approach to life is regarded as a survival strategy. This behaviour emerges as a reaction to regular adversities, and may be transposed to multiple environments. The brain neural circuits adapt in response to the adversities which can have a long-term impact upon brain architecture. Research highlights the generational impact: parent to child (Belsky & Pluess, 2009).

Early intervention

This inter-generational effect is addressed by services throughout the world today in a context of early intervention. Programmes may be formal or informal, and focus upon the creation of a therapeutic relationship between professional and parent as the medium for instigating change and development of parenting capacity (Whitters, 2015, 2016). Jester et al. (2009) compared executive functioning of different generations in families. Data had indicated a similar level of operational skill in relation to the mother, father and child. Recent research, conducted in the United States in 2017, found reciprocal links between parental responsiveness and a child's executive functioning (Merz et al., 2017). Research findings provide rationale for intervention which uses inter-generational learning. This approach has been shown to support development of families who are deemed to be at risk of negative impact upon attainment.

Key messages

- A child's executive functioning is nurtured within the context of a secure attachment relationship.
- The primary or secondary carer provides a role-model to the developing child through scaffolding knowledge, and extending learning at a pace

and manner which responds to each child's needs, abilities and also long- or short-term circumstances.
- Verbalising the child's emotions and tracking his actions supports an understanding of the autobiographical self and provides a route for external regulation to become internalised.
- Establishing appropriate methods of communication between child and adults/peers responds to additional support for learning needs and promotes inclusive pedagogy.
- Opportunities are offered to support lower and higher levels of functioning in a context of the five stages of self.
- Repetition of play is encouraged to promote the creation of skill-sets which are transferrable between activities.
- Up-regulation and down-regulation periods are incorporated within daily routines, and encourage the child's identification of personal strategies to support resilience, life-long learning and executive functioning.

Conclusion

This book has explored the concept of *executive functioning* in the early years from the perspective of research and practice. The term can appear unfamiliar to families who exist on the edges of society, and on the brink of child protection; however, parents have knowledge of executive functioning as these primary carers have an acute awareness of their children's interactions with the world. The associated concepts of "working memory," "response inhibition" and "task shifting" can appear unfamiliar to busy practitioners who are implementing curricula to infants; however, early years' workers have deep understanding of actualisation of achievement which can be demonstrated by a 10 month old as she masters a pop-up toy.

Research and practice are co-contributors to supporting attainment, and to creating an inclusive society. These concepts are activated in the diverse working environments of academia or services, and the implementation gap can be bridged by interested parties who actively seek to understand their own perspectives through the views of others. Terminology should not be regarded as a barrier to progress – academics and practitioners have equal responsibility to communicate with one another in order to merge theory and practice.

The expected outcome is to support all children to be independent learners, effective contributors and responsible citizens regardless of short- or long-term additional learning needs. Parents would agree with these aspirational goals and reference to the vernacular expressions of service-users can remind us why children deserve childhoods free from preventable adversities, rich in opportunities, happy in play, responsive in care, and in the words of a young father, "I want him to be all that he can be!"

Research and practice will continue to evolve and to marry theory with comprehension which informs actions in order to further the attainment of each generation. The attainment gap between parenting in a context of adversities, and projected national and international outcomes will continue to be highlighted and actioned through commissioning research. The disconnection between recommendations, and the magic of reciprocal learning in a context of secure attachment, will continue to be exposed and to be reduced through legislation, guidance and effective practitioners in the field.

The child's earliest years are a fascinating forum for a long vocational career. The global world is our workplace, and the child's world is our focus. As practitioners and researchers we must embrace progress, accept our fallibility as professional learners and continue to seek out knowledge, understanding and support from our extended teams in every community and country.

References

Belsky, J., & Pluess, M. (2009). Beyond diathesis stress: Differential susceptibility to environmental influences. *Psychological Bulletin, volume 135, number 6*. Retrieved on 1 May, 2017, from www.nhs.scot.knowledge.network

Belsky, J., & Pluess, M. (2013). Beyond risk, resilience, and dysregulation: Phenotypic plasticity and human development. *Development and Psychopathology, volume 25*, 1243–1261. Cambridge: Cambridge University Press.

Bodrova, E., Leong, D. J., & Akhutina, T. V. (2011). When everything new is well-forgotten old: Vygotsky/Luria insights in the development of executive functions. In R. M. Lerner, J. V. Lerner, E. P. Bowers, S. Lewin-Bizan, S. Gestsdottir & J. B. Urban (Eds.), *Thriving in childhood and adolescence: The role of self-regulation processes: New directions for child and adolescent development, volume 133* (pp. 11–28). San Francisco: Wiley Periodicals Inc.

Center on the Developing Child at Harvard University. (2017). *Toxic stress*. Retrieved on 21 June, 2018, from https://developing child.harvard.edu/science/key-concepts/toxic-stress/

Felitti, V. J., Anda, R. F., Nordenberg, D., Williamson, D. F., Spitz, A. M., Edwards, V., Koss, M. P., & Marks, J. S. (1998). Relationships of childhood abuse and household dysfunction to many of the leading causes of death in adults. *American Journal of Preventive Medicine, volume 14, number 4*. Retrieved on 25 December, 2017, from www.nhs.scot.knowledge.network

Heatherton, T. F., & Wagner, D. D. (2011). *Cognitive neuroscience of self-regulation failure*. Retrieved on 1 May, 2017, from www.nhs.scot.knowledge.network

Jester, J. M., Nigg, J. T., Puttler, L. I., Long, J. C., Fitzgerald, H. E., & Zucker, R. A. (2009). Intergenerational transmission of neuropsychological executive functioning. *Brain and Cognition, volume 70, number 1*. Retrieved on 7 December,

2017, from www.sciencedirect.com.knowledge.idm.oclc.org/science/article/pii/ S027826260

Merz, E. C., Landry, S. H., Montroy, J. J., & Williams, J. M. (2017). Bidirectional associations between parental responsiveness and executive function during early childhood. *Social Development, volume 26, number 3*. Retrieved on 28 May, 2018, from www.nhs.scot.knowledge.network

National Scientific Council on the Developing Child. (2014). *Excessive stress disrupts the architecture of the developing brain, working paper 3 updated*. Cambridge, MA: Harvard University Press.

Scottish Government. (2018). *What have ACEs got to do with justice?* Retrieved on 8 June, 2018, from www.gov.scot

Whitters, H. G. (2015). *Perceptions of the influences upon the parent-professional relationship in a context of early intervention and child protection*. Published doctoral thesis. Retrieved on 1 April, 2018, from the British Library http://ethos.bl.uk/OrderDetails.do?uin=uk.bl.ethos.655502

Whitters, H. G. (2016). *The parent-professional relationship in child protection*. Retrieved on 1 April, 2016, from withscotland.org/download/the-parent-professional-relationship-in-child-protection

Whitters, H. G. (2017). *Nursery nurse to early years' practitioner: Roles, relationships and responsibilities*. (pp. 26–29). Abingdon: Routledge.

Whitters. H. G. (2018). *Family learning to inclusion: Theory, practice and partnerships*. (pp. 18–22). Abingdon: Routledge.

Index

actualization 7
adulthood, stages of 2
adverse childhood experiences (ACEs) 74, 83
Aitken, K. J. 8
alert-inactivity 14
attachment figure, necessity of 52
attachment relationship and up-regulation 80
attachment theory 11–12, 15
attainment 84–85
attentive state 14
autobiographical self 1, 3; example from practice 23–24; intentional mental stage and 19–21; physical agent stage and 9–11; research and practice on 7–8; role-modelling and positive reinforcement and 23; scaffolding and 24; social agent stage and 11–16; stages of self and 8–9; teleological agent stage and 16–19; at three years of age 6–7

babbling 52
Basilio, M. 9, 10, 61
Bergen, D. 62
Bernier, A. 78
Bio-Ecological Theory of Human Development 16
Bowlby, J. 78
broadly congruent mirroring 42
Bronfenbrenner, U. 35

California Adverse Childhood Experience Study 12
cause and effect 19

Chabay, L. A. 54, 57
Children and Young People Act (Scotland) 27
children's learning understood developmentally 30–31
child's interest and attachment figure 20
classrooms as safe base 33–34
communication: all behaviour as 32–33; intra-personal and inter-personal (*see* intra-personal and inter-personal communication); language as vital means of 32–33; learning processes and 41–49; by primates 49–50
coping mechanisms 86
copying 42, 43–44
Craighero, L. 41, 44

daily routines 43–44
daily transitions 19–20
Daniels, H. 24
developmental plasticity 14
development of self: demonstrating an understanding of self and 23–24; intentional mental stage in 19–21; physical agent stage in 9–11; role-modelling and positive reinforcement in 21, 23; social agent stage in 11–16; stages in 8–21; supporting 23; teleological agent stage in 16–19
Diamond, A. 66, 67
double formation 54
down-regulation 78–80

Ecological Systems' Theory of Human Development 34

ego-centric speech 53
epigenetic change 15–16
executive functioning (EF) 1–2, 88–89; attachment relationship and up-regulation in 80; attainment and 84–85; defining 12, 66–67; inter-generational impact and (*see* inter-generational impact); response inhibition in 67, 70–74; rest and down-regulation in 78–80; self-regulation impairment and 74–76; task/set-shifting and 67, 76–78; working memory in 67–70
exo-systems 35
explicit memories 39, 68

family learning 84
Fay-Stammbach, T. 80
first and third generations of family, interaction between 11
Fischer, K. W. 70
Fonagy, P. 12, 32

Garon, N. 69, 71, 77
generations *see* inter-generational impact
gestures, private 58–61
Getting It Right for Every Child 34
Ghasemi, B. 61
Goldberg, M. E. 73

hand over hand teaching 44–49
Hashemi, M. 61
Heatherton, T. F. 83
Hegel, G. W. F. 18
Hencke, R. W. 70
Hofmann, W. 70, 77

Iguchi, Y. 76
implementation barrier 8
implementation gap 7–8; policy and 27–28; practice knowledge 28–29; research knowledge 29; theoretical principles in practice and 29–30; 21st century workforce and 28
implicit memories 68
inner speech 57
intelligence quotient (IQ) 66
intentional mental agent stage of self 19–21

inter-generational impact 8; adverse childhood experiences and 83; attainment and 84–85; early intervention for 87–88; epigenetic change and 15–16; family learning 84; interactions between first and third 11; stress 85–87
internalisation of language 53–54, 56–57
intra-personal and inter-personal communication: daily routines and sense of self in 43–44; example from practice 38–39; language acquisition and 61–64; learning processes in 41–49; mirror neurons and 41–42; motor action and language in 50–53; by primates 49–50; private gestures in 58–61; teaching and learning for 39–41; understanding the actions of others and 42; Vygotsky and internalisation of language in 53–54
Iverson, J. 50, 52

Kochanska, G. 69
Kuczynski, L. 69

language: acquisition of 61–64; functions of, in earliest years of childhood 54–55; internalisation of 53–54, 56–57; motor action and 50–53; private gestures in 58; self-regulation and 55
Lave, J. 42
law of double formation 54
learning processes: children's motor development and 52; daily routines and copying in 43–44; daily routines and working memory in 68–69; family learning 84; hand over hand teaching and 44–49; mirror neurons and 41–42; motor action and language in 50–53; motor patterns for 44, 46; necessity of attachment figure for 52; parents role in 50–51; in primates 49–50; promoting understanding of physical self 45–46; safe practice in 45; scaffolding in 24, 46; understanding the actions of others and 42
Lee, K. 66
local or cultural knowledge 42

Index

macro-systems 35
McCarthy, E. M. 54, 57
memories: explicit 39, 68; implicit 68
memory, working 67–70; toxic stress and 86
mental flexibility 67
mentalisation 18–19
micro-systems 35
mirror neurons 41–42
motor action and language 50–53

neurons, mirror 41–42
neuroplasticity 15, 84
new-born babies 9, 13–14
nurture importance for development of wellbeing 31–32
nurture principles 29–30; all behaviour is communication 32–33; children's learning understood developmentally 30–31; classroom offering safe base 33–34; importance of nurture for the development of wellbeing 31–32; importance of transition in children's lives 33–34; language as vital means of communication 32–33; professional reflection on 34–36

observation of children over time 33
overt speech 55–56

Palacios, P. 54, 58, 60, 63
Pauen, S. 66, 70, 79, 80
phonemes 61
physical agent stage of self 9–11
physical self, understanding of 45–46
Piaget, J. 53
Positive Parenting Programme (Triple P) 75
positive reinforcement of self 21, 23
positive stress 86
primates 49–50
private gestures 58–61
private speech 57

reaction to adversities 22; child's 21; primary carer's 20
research and practice on autobiographical self 7–8
resilience 31
response inhibition 67, 70–74

rest and down-regulation 78–80
Rizzolatti, G. 41, 44
Rodriguez, C. 54, 58, 60, 63
Rogers, S. J. 48
role-modelling 23
routines, daily 43–44; working memory and 68–69

safe practice 45
scaffolding 24, 46; working memory and 70
secure attachment 31–32
self, autobiographical *see* autobiographical self
self-control 67; effects of activation of 74–75; response inhibition and 72
self-reflection 35
self-regulation 2, 57, 67; impairment of 74–76; language and 55; response inhibition and 70–71, 72; tolerable stress and 86; tracking actions of self and others in 60–61
set-shifting 76–78
social agent stage of self 11–16
spread of affect 56
stages of self 8–9; intentional mental 19–21; physical agent 9–11; social agent 11–16; teleological agent 16–19
Stern, D. N. 8, 63
stress 85–87
strictly congruent initial mirroring 42

task/set-shifting 67, 76–78
teaching: communication in 39–41; hand over hand 44–49
teleological agent stage of self 16–19
Thought and Language 57
tolerable stress 86
toxic stress 86
tracking actions of self and others 60–61
transferrable skills 44
transitions: daily 19–20; importance of 33–34
Trevarthan, C. 8

understanding the actions of others 42
Universal Health Visiting Pathway, Scotland 27
up-regulation 80

visuo-motor cortex 44
Vivanti, G. 48
Vygotsky, L. 53–54, 55, 56, 57, 63, 77–78, 80

Wagner, D. D. 83
Weare, K. 34
wellbeing, importance of nurture for development of 31–32
Wenger, E. 42

Whitebread, D. 9, 10, 61
Wolff, P. H. 14
Woodin, M. 62
working memory 67–70

Yirka, B. 49

Zelazo, P. D. 78
zone of proximal development 77–78

For Product Safety Concerns and Information please contact our EU representative GPSR@taylorandfrancis.com
Taylor & Francis Verlag GmbH, Kaufingerstraße 24, 80331 München, Germany

www.ingramcontent.com/pod-product-compliance
Lightning Source LLC
Chambersburg PA
CBHW051758230426
43670CB00012B/2343